The Place of Morality
in Foreign Policy

Issues in World Politics Series

James N. Rosenau and William C. Potter, consulting editors

The Place of Morality in Foreign Policy

BY
Felix E. Oppenheim

Lexington Books

D.C. Heath and Company/Lexington, Massachusetts/Toronto

Library of Congress Cataloging-in-Publication Data

Oppenheim, Felix E., 1913–
   The place of morality in foreign policy / by Felix E. Oppenheim.
     p. cm.
   Includes bibliographical references and index.
   ISBN 0–669–21450–7. — ISBN 0–669–21452–3 (pbk.)
   1. International relations—Moral and ethical aspects. I. Title.
JX1255.066 1991
172'.4—dc 20   90-25426
                                                CIP

Published simultaneously in Canada
Printed in the United States of America
Casebound International Standard Book Number: 0–669–21450–7
Paperbound International Standard Book Number: 0–669–21452–3
Library of Congress Catalog Card Number: 90–25426

The paper used in this publication meets the minimum requirements
of American National Standard for Information Sciences—
Permanence of Paper for Printed Library Materials,
ANSI Z39.48–1984.

Year and number of this printing:

91 92 93 94 8 7 6 5 4 3 2 1

To my grandsons,
Noah, Nathan, Micah,
with the hope that their world
will have rendered this book obsolete

Contents

Preface

When is it relevant to judge foreign policies moral or immoral, and when are such judgments either redundant or counterproductive? This question should be asked first, before engaging in specific moral assessments. Therefore, answering this question is the object of the present study.

This book connects two disciplines: political science and philosophy. Hopefully, it will be of interest to the general reader, and especially to upper-level undergraduate and graduate students in moral and political philosophy as well as in international relations (to whom this series on Issues in World Politics is primarily addressed). For the sake of those in the latter field, I have avoided philosophical jargon (which should be dispensed with whenever possible), and have provided definitions for a few necessary technical terms.

My illustrations are chosen mainly, but not exclusively, from contemporary American foreign policy. My purpose is not to argue for or against these policies on either political or moral grounds. I do not lack strong convictions (the reader will have no difficulty reading between the lines to discover where I stand). Rather, my purpose in using these examples is to throw light on the question: do they fall within or outside the range of moral relevance?

I argue that there are objective criteria by which to answer this question, regardless of where one stands politically or morally. These criteria have to do with the rationality of a given policy in terms of the national interest. Here we come up against a difference in outlook between social scientists and philosophers. The former are likely to wonder: is it in any way possible to determine beforehand the overall balance between desirable and undesirable consequences of an agent's decision? How can one judge whether that decision is rational? More specifically, how can one ascertain whether a foreign policy–maker is guided by concern for the national interest or by other goals that may, or may not, be compatible with the former? How can one know whether a specific policy is rational in terms of the national interest? Political scientists tend therefore to be skeptical of the very use of such concepts as rationality and national interest. But moral philosophers, (especially those of the utilitarian persuasion) do not hesitate to define moral rightness in terms of the balance of good and bad consequences of actions, and rationality as the maximization of net expected utility. They are more likely to accept the concept of national interest as an objectively determinable end. In this respect, I lean toward the philosophical perspective. While acknowledging the difficulties, I try to convince political scientists that it is useful to avail ourselves of the concepts of rationality and national interest, taken in an objective sense, and that these concepts are indispensable for determining the place of morality in foreign affairs. With some luck, this approach will help bridge the gap between the two disciplines.

My interest in world politics has a personal basis. I grew up under the shadow of increasingly virulent German nationalism, culminating inevitably in Nazi ideology and power (often erroneously believed to be the sudden creation of a single man). I took comfort in the (all too feeble) affirmations of liberal welfare state philosophy made by Western democracies. Serving in the Belgian army, and then in the American army, the Second World War was to me a struggle between good and evil.

After World War II, when I noted that political rivalries between nations continued to be fought with ideological weapons, I gradually became more skeptical toward viewing foreign policy exclusively through moral lenses. Words were not matched by deeds, nor could they possibly be, and it would often have been unwise or even catastrophic if they had been. Yet, I felt that morality does have a place in foreign policy. These considerations prompted me to explore whether there is an objective way of determining the range of relevance of morality in this area. I arrived at the conclusion that the arena where morality does not enter extends further than is often assumed.

Some readers may be inclined to interpret this train of thought as an overreaction to my earlier idealistic inclinations, or as a manifestation of my European background. It is true that Europeans, because of their history and experience, are inclined to be more conscious of the realities of international power politics and more skeptical of official moral invocations. My wish is that this study be judged on the merits of its arguments, independently from these autobiographical factors.

Finding myself between two chairs, political science and philosophy, I was fortunate to benefit from the advice of colleagues sitting firmly on one or the other. James Rosenau and P. Terrence Hopmann in international relations and Thomas Pogge in philosophy gave me constructive criticism of an earlier draft. I also benefited from reactions to papers on the topic presented at the Yankee Conference on Political Thought, at a workshop of the European Consortium of Political Research (Amsterdam, 1987), and at the universities of Bologna, Florence, and Siena. My wife, Shulamith, helped me lighten the English without letting her own profession, writing children's tales, intrude on the grim realities of world politics. Having despaired of ever catching the computer's cursor, I turned to Doris Holden, who expertly converted the manuscript into final form. My thanks go to all.

Some sections of this study are based on my article "National Interest, Rationality, and Morality" (*Political Theory* 15 [1987]: 369–89).

Amherst, Massachusetts, November 1990

Introduction and Overview

What are some of the moral dilemmas associated with international politics? The following questions come immediately to mind: Do states have the moral right or duty to give primacy to their national interest? Do all states have this right, or only those states considered legitimate? What criteria determine legitimacy? Should governments subordinate their national interest to the promotion of such global goals as human rights or collective security or adequate living standards or clean environment? Ought foreign policies to aim primarily at the defense and diffusion of some ideology: free enterprise or communism, or national independence or religious fundamentalism? Is resorting to war ever morally justified? Do the ends in foreign policy justify whatever means are judged to be most effective? Is nuclear armament permissible, at least for the purpose of nuclear deterrence? Such questions have not diminished in importance with the end of the cold war, to judge by the pronouncements of public officials from countries around the globe.

It is not my purpose in this study to take sides. A more fundamental question must be asked first: Is it at all *relevant* to make moral judgments in this area and to address them to foreign policy decision makers? This, it seems to me, is *the* issue of morality in foreign policy. Indeed, there is no point in even asking questions such as those listed above unless they fall within the range of relevance. I believe that morality does have a place in foreign policy, but I also believe that its range of relevance is small. Yet, writers on ethics and international relations tend to commit themselves headlong to moral principles without considering the preliminary, and more fundamental, question of their relevance. It is this gap that the present study aims to fill.

In chapter 1, I shall explicate some basic concepts that will play key roles in the subsequent analysis. I shall point out in what sense *the state* can be considered as an *actor* on the international scene. The terms "self-interest" and "common interest" will help me define the key concept of *national interest*, whose pursuit must be distinguished from other foreign policy goals a state might adopt. This key concept will be defined in a way that will prove useful for the ensuing inquiry. The relevance of moral judgments in foreign policy has to do with the *rationality* of foreign policies. According to the instrumental view of rationality, intrinsic ends cannot be qualified as rational unless they are practically necessary (in a sense to be explained in chapter 2), but they may be subject to moral appraisal. While there is, in principle, a single set of criteria of rational choice, there are various, and conflicting, points of view concerning *morality*. Without getting involved in metaethical discussions, my position will be in agreement with the thesis that there are no objective criteria by which to resolve intrinsic moral conflicts.

Chapter 2 applies the criteria of rationality to the choice of foreign policy goals, in order to determine the place of morality in foreign policy, the subject of chapter 3. One criterion will prove to be particularly important: It is rational to adopt a goal that, while theoretically avoidable, is practically necessary (in a sense to be specified), and it is not rational to pursue a goal that is, for all practical purposes, unavailable. Given our present system of independent states-as-actors, it is practically necessary, and hence rational, for any state to pursue its own national interest, and practically impossible, and hence not rational, to adopt foreign policy goals incompatible with its national interest. This aspect of international relations will be contrasted with domestic politics, where government usually has a practical choice, for example, to promote either some collective welfare goal or the particular interest of various groups. For the latter, the national interest is not a practically necessary goal.

In chapter 3 I turn to the relevance of moral judgments for the adoption of foreign policy goals. Moral utterances in this area are typically addressed to government officials either with the aim of influencing them to adopt ends judged morally right or to criticize them for having chosen immoral goals. I interpret the adage that "'ought' implies 'can'" in the pragmatic sense that it is relevant to advise someone that he ought to act in a certain way only if he can do so, in a practical as well as in a strict sense. Accordingly, there is no point in judging the adoption of a practically necessary or practically unavailable goal as either right or wrong. Since the pursuit of the national interest is a practical necessity for statesmen, it is of no avail to advise them that they ought, or that they ought not, to do so on moral grounds. That it is rational to aim at securing the national interest does not involve any celebration of nationalism. Urging foreign policy–makers to adopt some goal incompatible with the national interest is advising them not to act rationally. Sometimes, the national interest and our moral convictions coincide. Cooperation for common purposes, for example, generally considered right, is often rational with respect to the national interest. More often, national interest goals are covered up by moralizing rhetoric. Moral judgments are relevant when a government is faced with the decision whether to adopt a foreign policy goal *compatible* with its national interest. I shall give examples of possible goals consistent with the necessary goal of the national interest, but it is not the purpose of this study to make explicit judgments of moral approbation or disapproval, as it is concerned with determining the extent to which moral judgments in this area are relevant.

Chapter 4 inquires into the relevance of moral judgments for specific policies aimed at securing the national interest. If there is a choice between several alternative strategies, it is appropriate to recommend or to oppose one or some of them on moral grounds. But, it is redundant to recommend the most effective or the only suitable policy as morally right; and to oppose such a policy on moral grounds is to favor one lacking rationality. Policies that are, with respect to the national interest, rational are sometimes considered moral, sometimes immoral, and the same holds true for policies failing the test of rationality. The four situations will be illustrated by examples, but again I will not take sides.

The previous considerations will be applied to military matters in the last two chapters. Under what conditions is it relevant to consider resort to war just or unjust? When is it appropriate to judge methods of warfare right or wrong? Can nuclear deterrence be justified or condemned on moral grounds?

The critical discussion of the views expressed by many moralists on threatening, initiating, and waging war will support the main conclusion of this study: the range of relevance of moral judgments about foreign policy goals and foreign policies in view of such goals is much narrower than often assumed. I hope that this conclusion will motivate moral thinkers to restrict themselves to the range where their moral judgments can have some effect on foreign policy decision making.

1
Some Basic Concepts

To what extent is morality relevant for making foreign policy decisions? This is the fundamental issue I intend to examine in this study. Four basic concepts will be used to deal with this controversy.

1. The State as Actor

Generally, terms such as "right" and "wrong", "moral" and "immoral" refer to characteristics of actions, while terms such as "good" and "desirable" refer to outcomes of actions. At the level of international relations, actions and their outcomes, judged on moral grounds, are principally foreign policies, enacted or contemplated by government officials in their role as foreign policy decision makers.

Strictly speaking, only individuals desire, prefer, choose, decide, and act. Yet, we speak of actions taken by groups: Congress enacts a bill, the Catholic church opposes abortion, Solidarity forms a Polish government, the United Nations censures Israel. The state, too, can be conceived as acting, on foreign as well as on domestic matters: we say, for example, that the United States might increase its foreign aid, that Spain joined the European Economic Community, that the Soviet Union invaded Afghanistan, and we judge such state actions as morally right or wrong. It is legitimate to conceptualize the state as an actor on the international scene, provided that we are aware that we are speaking metaphorically, that we are, strictly speaking, referring to the actions of persons who are acting on behalf of the state.[1] "Acts of the state are acts of persons in an official capacity, acting according to procedures and within the competence prescribed by the rules of its constitution" (Benn 1967, 7). Attributes of persons such as belief, preference, and will cannot be ascribed to the state in a literal sense. To do so would be to invite the danger of conceiving the state as an organism, endowed with a "general will" different from, and "superior" to, the preferences of its individual members.

On the other hand, to say that, strictly speaking, only individuals act, and that states act only metaphorically, does not imply that "only individuals really exist," not states (Gilpin 1986, 318). This is like saying that trees really exist, but forests do not really exist. "Forest" and "state" are theoretical terms, but so are "tree" and "individual"—all four terms are linguistic constructs for the purpose of convenient communication; what they refer to may or may not exist. "Ruritania does not exist, but France does" (Parfit 1986, 211). Nor does the assertion that the state acts only in a figurative sense commit one to the reductionist view that all group properties are definable in terms of attributes of their individual members, and that all group phenomena are explainable by reference to the attributes of their individual constituents. They are not. For example, a *democracy* is a system of democratic institutions (such as periodic, free elections), not an aggregate of persons holding democratic convictions. The United States is defined by its geography, history, political structure, legal institutions—characteristics that cannot be attributed to individual Americans. We shall see that the collective interest of a group need not correspond to the self-interest of its members, and that a foreign policy aimed at the protection of national security (i.e., the security of the state) need not be in the interest of all its citizens.

"Proclaiming the state as a singular actor with a unified set of objectives" has been criticized as "one of the unexamined assumptions from which theoretical discourse proceeds" in the field of international politics (Ashley 1986, 270). Conceptualizing (not "proclaiming") the state as actor is not making "one of the unexamined assumptions," but constructing a *model*. Models are "systems that deliberately simplify and even falsify the empirical situation under investigation for purposes of convenience in research or application" (Hesse 1967, 355). The model of classical mechanics, for example, makes the *counterfactual* assumption of the absence of air pressure. The model of classical economics is based on the simplifying hypothesis that business firms aim solely at maximizing their profits. The state-as-actor, too, is a model. "In defining international-political structures we take states with whatever traditions, habits, objectives, desires, and forms of governments they may have" (Waltz 1979, 99). To adopt the model of international relations as a system of interacting states is not to deny that foreign policies are in fact often the outcome of domestic political pressures. Yet, definite foreign policies of the state finally emerge. The question is, to what extent are they subject to moral evaluation?

The state-as-actor model has been linked to the "state-centric" conception of international politics, the view that the state is the only significant actor on the stage of world politics. It has been pointed out that

> activity in the global community today is the result not only of nation-states striving for goals, but also of a number of varied transnational collectivities—from multinational corporations to professional societies to international organizations to terrorists and so on through a vast range of new kinds of actors— engaging in pursuits that are not confined to national boundaries. (Rosenau 1989, 5)

The United Nations secretary general, for example, has often successfully mediated disputes between states. On the other hand, resolutions of the United Nations General Assembly are the outcomes of votes by member states (actually, their delegates), and such recommendations are not binding. "In a world of nation states, international organizations tend to reflect the power and interests of the dominant states in the international system" (Gilpin 1981, 410). Multinational corporations frequently make decisions directly affecting international relations, yet they are themselves subject to the control of governments in whose territory they operate (by means of export licenses, taxation, tariffs, etc.). No doubt, some transnational organizations like the United Nations or the European Community and even some multinational corporations such as IBM or Volkswagen are more significant than some states, say Chad or San Marino.

I need not take sides in the controversy of the relative importance of states and of transnational collectivities because my reason
for adopting the state-as-actor model has nothing to do with that
issue, but is instead determined by the topic of this study. It so
happens that moral thinkers about international politics have been
dealing primarily, if not exclusively, with such questions as whether
it is right or wrong for *states* to care foremost for their national
interest, or to what extent foreign policies of *states* in view of this
goal can be qualified as right or wrong. This is not to deny that
United Nations resolutions, such as the recent condemnation of
Iraq's aggression against Kuwait, often have substantial moral
impact on a variety of international situations or that the decisions
of multinational corporations may have consequences posing
moral questions (e.g., the disaster caused by Union Carbide in
India or the sale of baby formula by Nestlé in third world
countries).

2. The National Interest

The basic question of ethics applied to foreign policy *goals* is: Are
states morally entitled to aim primarily at the pursuit of their
national interest, or ought they to subordinate the national interest to other ends such as promoting some universal cause? Hence,
it is necessary to define the concept of national interest, keeping in
mind that definitions of this kind are not to be judged as true or
false; they are mere linguistic stipulations adopted for their
usefulness in specific contexts.

Self-interest

The concept of self-interest is important in its own right, and also
because of its connection with the concept of national interest.
What meaning should we attach to the expression, "It is in the self-
interest of A (a person or group) to do X, or to aim at X"? Clearly,
this statement is not synonymous with "A wants X"; otherwise, it
would be logically excluded for an agent to desire what is not in
his interest[2]—for example, one could not say, "John wants drugs,
but it is not in his self-interest to have drugs." Intuitively, we

would hardly consider an action to be in the agent's self-interest unless it is *rational* for him to perform it. Acting rationally (in a sense soon to be clarified) is the first defining characteristic of the concept of interest, including such related concepts as self-interest and national interest.

But surely, "self-interest" does not refer to acting rationally in view of whatever goal one might adopt. The concept must be narrowed down further to designate particular kinds of goals, namely welfare goals.[3] "Well-being" or "welfare" or "utility"[4] in turn should be defined neither too narrowly nor too broadly. Not too narrowly: the concept refers not just to material goods or wealth, but to material advantages in a broader sense, including such things as health and personal security.[5] Not too broadly: "welfare" applies only to material advantage, not, for example, to the psychological gratification someone might derive from a more just distribution of wealth. Dissidents voicing their opposition to the totalitarian regime under which they live do not act in their self-interest, but for the purpose of promoting some cause or upholding some principle.

Accordingly, I propose to define the expression "Doing X is in A's self-interest" by "It is rational for A to do X with respect to some welfare goal of his" (cf. Oppenheim 1981, 123–34).

Common Interest

Acting in one's own interest must be distinguished from furthering the interest of others (i.e., promoting their well-being), possibly at the expense of one's own interest. When Saint Francis of Assisi distributed his own wealth to the poor, he did so to promote *their* well-being; and since his action was rational in view of that goal, he acted in *their* interest.

More important for our topic is the distinction between acting in one's own interest or pursuing the common interest of a group to which one belongs. We have seen that, literally, only individuals choose and act, and that groups do so only metaphorically. But groups as well as individuals can have interests, literally. Interest groups such as trade unions, churches, universities, and political parties have common interests; that is, welfare goals that it is in the group's common interest to pursue.

> The notion of something's being in one's interest . . . which we
> attribute to individuals, is also applied to groups in situations
> where they stand to benefit from a course of action or events.
> Thus a general rise in the standard of living might be said to be in
> the interest of the working class, and on the basis of such
> examples we might conclude that something is in the interest of a
> group when it is in the interests of its members. (James 1984, 47)

But such common interests are not necessarily in the interest of all
its members. It is in the common interest of a group like the state
to procure public goods[6] such as cleaner air, and it may therefore
be rational for its government to enact and to enforce antipollution
legislation in view of this collective welfare goal. However, it may
be in the self-interest of each member of the group that all others
contribute to its production, but that each member be a free-rider
(i.e., to benefit from a public good while avoiding any share of the
costs for that good), as long as there is a high probability that the
public good will be produced without his contribution.[7] This is the
problem of the "prisoner's dilemma," which will concern us later
when we deal with the problem of the rationality of states cooperating for some common purpose, and with the question of whether
such cooperation is to be considered a moral duty.

Acting self-interestedly, acting in the interest of others, acting
in the common interest—all these interest goals must be distinguished from non–welfare goals such as the promotion of some
cause such as human rights or religious fundamentalism.[8]

National Interest

The proposed definitions of *self-interest* and *common interest* will
help to clarify the notion of *national interest*. Often considered
too vague and ambiguous for analytic purposes, the concept can
be made useful here if it is given a precise meaning.

First, "national" is somewhat misleading. As mentioned, international relations, and moral judgments in this field, are concerned
primarily with the actions and interactions of existing states. States
can be made up of various nations (e.g., the Soviet Union); moreover, some nations aspire to become states (e.g., the Poles during
much of their history, Palestinians today). But we are not dealing
here with the interest of the Kurds or the Armenians or the Pales-

tinians to form their own state or with their right to independence. Our concern is with the foreign policies of existing states. For this reason, the term "national interest" will be taken as referring to the interest not of a nation, but of a state.

States are actors, figuratively speaking; but like groups in general states can have interests, literally speaking. "States can be agents and can have ends. Like persons, they also can have interests" (McMahan 1986, 29).[9] As with "self-interest" and "common interest," I am taking "national interest" as referring to welfare goals. More precisely, the national interest comprises the following collective welfare goals a state might pursue by means of its foreign policies: its territorial integrity (or political sovereignty), its military security, and its economic well-being. There are also, of course, domestic collective welfare goals; one may say, for example, that it is in the national interest to increase taxation to improve public education. It has become customary, however, to use the term "public interest" when dealing with domestic matters, and to restrict the term "national interest" to goals and policies at the international level (cf. Rosenau 1968, 35). Accordingly, that it is in the national interest of a certain state to adopt a certain foreign policy means that it is rational for its government to adopt it in view of these collective welfare goals.

On the basis of the proposed definition, we can ask such questions as: Did the United States, during its conflict with Vietnam, pursue its national interest, or was its primary purpose to "combat world communism"? Is it in the national interest of the United States to provide economic aid to underdeveloped countries? That is to say, is it rational for the United States to adopt this policy in view of its own economic well-being?

Let me emphasize that the judgment "It is in the national interest to adopt this foreign policy" does not indicate anything about whether the government actually does act in the national interest. If the national interest were whatever foreign policy-makers decide it to be, it would be logically impossible for states to act contrary to their national interest. Nor can the national interest be conceived in terms of the outcome of the political process. A state's foreign policy decisions are often influenced by groups wielding power over government or, in democratic countries, by public opinion-at-large. Policies are frequently claimed to be in the national interest when they fail to be rational with respect to, say, the national security. During the Cuban missile crisis, President Kennedy was under pressure, especially from the Republican party, to launch a conventional, if not a nuclear, attack against the island. Sound advice finally prevailed, and he settled for a naval blockade, a rational policy under the circumstances. This is not to deny that there can be reasonable disagreement on such matters. Even so, the underlying assumption is that it is, at least in principle, possible to determine the national interest by objective criteria.

Admittedly, this raises many questions that cannot easily be answered. Since the national interest is not just whatever the government says it is, who decides whether a proposed or adopted foreign policy is "really" in the national interest? How do we know whether a statesman does aim at the pursuit of the national interest or has adopted some different goal? Was America's reaction against Iraq after its invasion of Kuwait prompted by the desire to "do what's right" or to ensure "the free flow of oil at tolerable prices"? Is the national interest compatible with promoting some cause? There was, no doubt, a coincidence between the national interests of Great Britain and of the United States and the goal of upholding the "four freedoms" during the Second World War. On the other hand, combating "world communism" in Vietnam has been judged by many to have been detrimental to American national interest. How is one to balance short-range versus long-range national interests? Does not the concept of the national interest presuppose, at least implicitly, some Platonic philosopher-king who "knows" beyond the shadows what the national interest consists of and what policies are required to implement it? Many writers in the field of international relations have concluded, with James Rosenau,

> that the national interest has not sparked research or otherwise lived up to its early promise as an analytic tool . . . [because the concept] suffer[s] from difficulties which defy resolution and which confound rather than clarify analysis. (Rosenau 1968, 39)

I am far from minimizing these difficulties. Why then adopt the national interest as one of the basic concepts necessary for this study? Because I consider this notion, like that of the state-as-actor, useful, and even indispensable, for my discussion. It captures the distinction, of primary importance to moralists, between collective welfare goals and non material aims, such as the promotion of some ideological or religious cause, that a state might adopt in its foreign policy. The proposed definition enables us to formulate the very questions of primary concern to moral philosophy: Is the pursuit of the national interest legitimate for every state, or only for democratic states, or only for a particular state? Or do states have the moral duty to adopt goals different from, and possibly in conflict with, their national interest?

The following definition captures this difference, but only in part: "The concept of the national interest is, practically by definition, an idea based on nondistributive, indivisible values, enjoyed by society as a whole: security, prestige, territoriality" (Hanrieder 1981, 140). For reasons already indicated, "prestige" had better be left out, as it does not constitute a *material* public good. A country risking war for the sake of prestige may endanger its national security and thus its national interest. In 1962, for example, Krushchev ordered the building of ballistic missile sites in Cuba, evidently to give the *appearance* of altering the strategic balance with the United States. John F. Kennedy's goal was to avoid a nuclear exchange *without losing face,* so he imposed "a strict quarantine on all offensive military equipment" being shipped to Cuba. Both sides realized that it was *contrary to their respective national interests* to risk nuclear war and, possibly, mutual annihilation. "The most serious crisis in the history of mankind, in short, turned on a question of appearances. The world came close to total destruction over a matter of prestige" (Ambrose 1988, 193). But the definition of national interest should include "economic well-being," not of particular individuals or groups within a state, but as a collective good of the state itself, and in the sense of maintaining it at its existing level, as distinguished from increasing it at the expense of other states. Thus one can ask whether American economic policy regarding Japan is in America's national interest or only works for the economic advantage of certain American firms?

The crucial distinction I wish to make is also blurred if the concept of national interest is equated with the ambiguous notion of survival. "Suppose the national interest is defined in terms of national survival. . . . It seems beyond dispute that it is the survival of values and not simply of human beings which is at stake" (Hare & Joynt 1982, 48). "National interest," as defined here, refers to various public goods, among them sometimes the survival of the *state* in the sense of its ability to maintain national independence. This goal may require sacrificing human beings (in a defensive war) or relinquishing territory (e.g., France's decision to grant independence to Algeria) or merging with other states to form a larger confederation (e.g., the European Economic Community). The distinction between the national interest as a public good and the values that the pursuit of the national interest sometimes promotes will be of cardinal importance for our topic.

As the definition just criticized illustrates, the term *national interest* has a positive valuational connotation, and the *concept* of national interest is therefore often taken, in a normative sense, to refer to whatever foreign policy the speaker happens to advocate: "What is to count as [national] self-interest is partially determined by normative considerations: . . . that this particular interest ought to be recognized as a *legitimate* one, as one which ought to be defended" (Frost 1986, 9–10). Such language gives license to favor whatever policy the speaker believes "ought to be defended" under the guise of the national interest. Hence, "analysts have discovered that the value-laden character of the concept makes it difficult to employ as a tool for rigorous investigation" and that it therefore "has lost some of its early appeal as an analytic tool" (Rosenau 1968, 34). The proposed, valuationally neutral definition enables us to determine the national interest objectively—at least in principle.

The national interest can be considered from either an internal or an external point of view. *Internally,* a foreign policy may promote the national interest or the interest of particular groups. But it does not follow that "the diversity of interests pursued by such groups belies the myth of *a* national interest" (Alger 1981, 177). That groups often pursue their divergent self-interests does not indicate that the national interest is a "myth." It is a reality in the sense of a collective good, and as such a possible foreign policy goal. To postulate that it is in the national interest of the United States not to raise tariffs or quotas against Japanese cars is not to deny that this policy may be contrary to the self-interest of

General Motors or of the United Automobile Workers Union. Nor does the *concept* of the national interest imply that there always *is* a common interest. For example, a falling dollar helps American exporters but hurts the interest of American importers.

I will be concerned mainly with national interest in its *external* aspects. Viewing the state as a unitary actor, the statement "It is in the national interest of the United States to increase economic aid to Eastern Europe" means that this policy is in America's *self-interest,* and only incidentally in the interest of Eastern European countries or in compliance with humanitarian principles.

To recapitulate: Foreign policies are enacted, strictly speaking, by individuals on behalf of the state, and, figuratively speaking, by the state itself. A state's foreign policy sometimes aims at securing its national interest, from an internal point of view a *collective welfare goal* of the state, from an external point of view a goal that it is in a state's *self-interest* to adopt.

3. Rationality

The concept of rationality is important, not only because it refers to one of the defining characteristics of self-interest or national interest, but also because the relevance of moral judgments about foreign policies depends on whether criteria of rationality are applicable.

I use "rationality" in the sense of "instrumental rationality," the appropriateness of means to an agent's ends, whatever they may be, in contradistinction to the view that intrinsic ends or desires themselves can be said to be rational or not.[10] "The term 'rational' denotes behavior that is appropriate to specific goals in the context of a given situation" (Simon 1985, 294), "behavior involving a choice of the best *means* to achieve a given end" (Harsanyi 1985, 42). For my purposes here, it is not necessary to enter into the technicalities of the theory of rational choice. Suffice it to say that, given an agent's goal, and given the information available to him in a specific situation, his action is rational if it is the optimal means to achieve the given goal. To that effect, the agent must determine what alternative courses of action are open to him, predict their probable outcomes, assess their relative desirability to him, and select the option with his preferred outcome. As it is generally put, an actor acts rationally if he maximizes his net expected utility, where "utility" is taken in the broad sense of satisfaction of the actor's preferences, whatever they may be. For example, some hold that, given the goal of maintaining peace, unilateral disarmament is rational, while others consider this policy unsuitable to achieving that end. Whether this policy is rational *can in principle* be determined objectively, by estimating the relative probability of avoiding war as a result of unilateral disarmament against the probability of adopting a different policy, such as maintaining military parity.

Accordingly, given *any* goal, it is in principle possible to determine whether a certain course of action is rational in terms of that goal. One can go about rationally or not rationally buying stocks, robbing a bank, protecting national security, or subjugating another country. Acting rationally does not imply acting self-interestedly.[11] When Saint Francis distributed his wealth to the poor, he acted rationally in view of his altruistic goal of promoting the well-being of the poor. It would not be rational for citizens under a dictatorship to criticize the regime if they aim at advancing in the bureaucracy, but it would be rational if their goal is to uphold the principle of basic liberties. A foreign aid policy may be rational from the point of view of relieving world hunger, but not rational with respect to the national interest (but usually both goals are compatible, as we shall see).

That one can act rationally in terms of goals other than self-interest constitutes an implicit refutation of the claim that the instrumental view of rationality is linked to "possessive individualism" and laissez-faire capitalism, a view held by Macpherson (1973, 199). Nor is the instrumental view of rationality tied to psychological egoism, the—surely mistaken— theory that "human nature" is basically egoistic, calculating, materialistic, competitive. Anyhow, I am dealing with the conditions under which actions are to be considered rational, not with the actual motives of people's (including statesmen's) behavior.

Rational choice theory "tells us what we ought to do in order to achieve our aims as well as possible. It does not tell us what our aims ought to be" (Elster 1989, 3). Suppose a person is confronted with the choice between promoting the well-being of others or his own well-being, or that a government has the choice of devoting a fixed amount of its budget either to promoting the standard of living in the third world or to domestic welfare. According to the instrumental theory, it is not possible to qualify the adoption of either goal itself as either rational or not.[12] Choosing an intrinsic goal can be said to be nonrational, whereas the choice of a means to a given goal is, in principle, either rational or not rational.[13]

The thesis that the adoption of an intrinsic end is nonrational does not imply, however, that criteria of rationality are applicable only to means to given ends. Here are some examples of processes of choosing intrinsic goals that are not rational:

1. Failure to be aware of all available ends. "People often *overlook* goals they might pursue if they thought of them" (Putnam 1981, 169).

2. Underestimating the opportunity costs of reaching one's goal. For example, a more egalitarian society, realizable only by revolution, may foreseeably involve more bloodshed than acceptable to the revolutionaries themselves.

3. Misjudging one's "real" preferences. (That is why interest statements do not refer to what the actor happens to "want.")

4. Espousing incompatible goals; for example, promoting democracy abroad *and* abiding by the principle of noninterference with the internal matters of other states.

5. Adopting some utopian goal (not even in theory attainable by any available means); for example, a world federation at the present time.

6. Selecting practically impossible goals. (I shall define this concept later, and deal specifically with practically impossible and practically necessary foreign policy goals. The thesis will be that it is practically necessary, and hence rational, for states to pursue their national interest—an important exception to the principle that criteria of rationality are inapplicable to the choice of intrinsic goals.)

The instrumental view of rationality has often been challenged. To take a recent example:

> The rational person is not constituted by whatever ends or preferences he happens to have at any given moment. Rationality consists, at least partly, in our capacity to make our ends and preferences the object of rational consideration and to revise them in accordance with reasons we find compelling. (Darwall 1983, 101)

In the same vein, Richard Brandt speaks of the rationality of "a basic or intrinsic desire, aversion, or preference" (Brandt 1977, 268). The view that intrinsic goals are subject to rational assessment is linked, at least implicitly, to the philosophy of valuational and moral cognitivism, which maintains that intrinsic value judgments are in principle true or false, and demonstrably so. I do not subscribe to this philosophy, as I shall point out in the next section. I maintain that the adoption of an intrinsic goal cannot be qualified as either rational or not rational, with the exception—important for our subject—that it is rational to adopt practically necessary goals. This topic will be discussed in chapter 2.

4. Morality

"A moral or ethical statement may assert that some particular action is right or wrong, . . . or it may propound some broad principle from which more detailed judgments of these sorts might be inferred" (Mackie 1977, 9). An ethical statement in the area of international politics may proclaim the general moral principle that it is permissible (or obligatory) for states to pursue their national interest, or that it is wrong to do so if such action violates the duty to respect the norms of international law. From the former principle we can derive (together with certain other, empirical premises) that it is right for the United States to conclude reduction of armaments agreements with Soviet Russia, from the latter that Iraq's annexation of Kuwait was wrong.

"Morality must be contrasted with prudence" (Frankena 1973, 7). An action may be rational, yet immoral, that is, contrary to *some* standard of morality. There is, in principle, one standard of rationality, but there are various, and conflicting, moral points of view that have been propounded in different cultures and within the same society by different individuals or groups. A course of action meeting all criteria of rational choice may be considered immoral (e.g., free riding, attacking another country). Means consistent with (but not indispensable to) a given goal may be judged wrong (e.g., war atrocities) even if the end itself is considered right (e.g., in a "just war"). Choosing between alternative intrinsic ends, while not subsumable under the criterion of rationality, may be subject to moral appraisal (e.g., promoting human rights internationally). The reverse holds when it comes to adopting a practically necessary goal. Such conduct, while rational, is not subject to moral appraisal (for reasons to be given in chapter 3).

Can conflicts between different moral points of view be resolved? This is a question relating to the logic of moral discourse, and belongs to moral philosophy. The philosophy of ethical cognitivism holds that some intrinsic moral principles are demonstrably either true or false. For example, moral cognitivists often single out as objectively valid the principle that it is obligatory for everyone to pursue the common good, and wrong to act self-interestedly at its expense. According to ethical noncognitivism, utterances of intrinsic moral principles reflect the speaker's subjective moral commitments, and there are no objective criteria by which to decide between conflicting moral points of view.

As mentioned before, ethical cognitivists affirm that criteria of rationality also apply to intrinsic moral judgments, and that it is therefore rational to comply with objectively valid moral injunctions. Noncognitivists deny these affirmations. On the other hand, there is no disagreement between these two metaethical schools about the logic of extrinsic (or instrumental) ethical judgments (i.e., of judgments about the adequacy of means to given ends). These are judgments of instrumental rationality, and they are without doubt in principle either true or false.

Here is not the place to enter into the age-old metaethical controversy between moral cognitivists and noncognitivists. I have indicated elsewhere (Oppenheim 1976) why I believe that the cognitivists have not been successful in defending their thesis, while noncognitivists have shown that intrinsic moral principles are a matter of subjective commitment.

There are deontological and consequential systems of ethics (cf. Frankena 1973, 15–17). Deontological ethics considers it morally obligatory to act in conformity with certain general moral principles, whatever the consequences (e.g., always to comply with treaty obligations, or always to respect the rules of just war). According to consequentialism, the rightness or wrongness of an action depends on the balance of positive over negative value of its total predicted outcome.[14]

Consequentialist ethical theories can in turn be subdivided as follows:

Egoism: Individuals may or ought to promote their own interest, and states their national interest.

Altruism: Individuals have the moral duty to further the interest of others (sometimes at the expense of their own), and states to subordinate their own national interest to that of some other state or states.

Benevolence: One ought to promote the common interest of one's group, and states should act in the interest they have in common with other states, even at the expense of their own short-term interest.

In our Western tradition, egoism has most often been considered wrong, and it has been judged moral to further the interest of others or to act in the common interest or to comply with general deontological principles. To give a modern example of this view: "To act for reasons of morality is to act, not out of self-interest, but out of an intrinsic concern and respect for people as 'ends in themselves'" (Harman 1977, 151). "Moral," like "rational" or "national interest," has a positive valuational connotation, at least in our culture; hence, the tendency to apply these terms only to norms that happen to correspond to the speaker's preferences. Yet the morality of egoism, too, has had a long tradition, although more in practice than in theory, especially in the form of elitism, the view that certain persons or groups are entitled to promote their self-interests and all others have the duty to serve the interests of the former. I shall deal in chapter 3 with the theory that a state is morally entitled to pursue its national interest, and distinguish it from other moral points of view concerning foreign policy goals.

In this introductory chapter, I have attempted to define certain basic concepts in order to make them suitable for the subsequent analysis. For that purpose, it seems useful to consider the *state as actor* in world politics, because ethics applied to international relations is primarily concerned with the foreign policies of states. More specifically, ethics deals with the question whether states are morally entitled to pursue above all their *national interest,* or whether governments ought to adopt different ultimate goals. To clarify this dilemma, it is practical to restrict the concept of the national interest to certain collective welfare goals: territorial integrity, national security, collective economic well-being.

There is an important relationship between the *rationality* of a state's foreign policies and the relevance of moral judgments in this area. According to the instrumental view of rationality, an action or policy is rational if it is the optimal means to achieve the agent's goal; but the choice of an intrinsic goal is nonrational. (However, it will be shown that it is rational to adopt a practically necessary end.) By contrast, standards of *morality* are applicable to ultimate ends as well as to means. I subscribe to the moral philosophy that intrinsic moral judgments are not demonstrably true or false, but express subjective moral commitments and attitudes.

Notes

1. "Theories about the behaviour of some classes of social wholes may begin, then, by taking predicates which are usually applied to individuals and extending them in a *metaphorical* fashion to groups" (James 1984, 48; italics supplied).
2. No sexist prejudice should be inferred from my using throughout "his" to stand for "his" or "her," and "he" for "he" or "she." I do so for the sake of convenience.
3. "[O]ne's interests are at most a subclass of one's wants, namely what one wants and needs for one's well-being" (White 1975, 119). "Self-interest is an interest in the well-being of the particular person that is oneself" (Wolf 1986, 706).
4. "'Utility' can serve as a convenient shorthand for well-being" (Sen 1987, 40).
5. Interest "always appears to have carried an emphasis on material advantage" (Barry & Rae 1975, 382). "'Welfare' is a convoy concept" that may include such things as "food; safety; clothing; shelter; medical care; . . . congenial employment; companionship" (Braybrooke 1968, 143).

6. Goods "which any member of the public may benefit from, whether or not he or she contributes in any way to their provision" (Taylor 1987, 15). Classical examples are a lighthouse, a park, police protection, national defense.

7. That the common interest of a group cannot be defined as the sum of self-interests of its members is an argument against the thesis of reductionism, the claim that statements about collectivities can be translated into statements about their individual members.

8. "A person may value the promotion of certain causes and the occurrence of certain things, even though the importance that is attached to these developments are not reflected by the advancement of his or her well-being" (Sen 1987, 40).

9. For the opposite view, that states, and groups generally, do not have interests, see Gilpin 1986, 317.

10. "One's not obtaining because the wanted event is thought to be a means to the satisfaction of another desire" (Brandt 1990, 262).

11. "By acting rationally . . . we assure that our desires . . . are satisfied as fully as possible in the circumstances, *irrespective of what they are*" (Brandt 1979, 154; italics added). "It is irrational to do what is in our own self-interest when we know that it will frustrate what, knowing the facts and thinking clearly, we most want and value" (Parfit 1986, 194).

12. "The choice of 'ends' or 'goals' is *neither rational nor irrational* (provided some minimal consistency requirements are met); while the choice of means *is rational to the extent that it is efficient*" (Putnam 1981, 168).

13. The term "irrational" had better be avoided here, because acting irrationally has the connotation of acting emotionally rather than reasonably.

14. Social scientists are likely to wonder: How does one estimate the balance between the positive and negative values or goodness of the overall consequences of a contemplated action? And by what standards of value? The difficulty is similar to the problem of determining the rationality of an action by asking whether it is most likely to maximize the agent's net expected utility, or of finding out whether a proposed foreign policy is most likely to maximize the national interest. Philosophers, on the other hand, have been using such concepts without hesitation in spite of these difficulties. Here is a difference in outlook, and hence a difficulty of communication, between the two disciplines that this study is trying to bridge.

2
Rationality and Foreign Policy Goals

Whether it is relevant to call the adoption of a certain foreign policy goal or of a certain foreign policy morally right or wrong depends in part on whether the criteria of rational choice are applicable. The present chapter examines the conditions under which foreign policy goals are rational; chapter 4 will deal with the rationality of specific foreign policies.

1. Anarchical Character of the World Political System

For the purpose of the topic, it is best to concentrate on states as "the units whose interactions form the structure of world politics" (Waltz 1979, 95). In the historical era in which we live, this structure is essentially anarchical. This is not a contradiction in terms, provided we do not take *anarchical* to mean "disorderly" or "chaotic," but use the term in its original Greek sense of "absence of rule." Whereas actors within a state can in many cases be forced to cooperate (e.g., to comply with legal enactments) by a central government, states-as-actors are not subject to a supranational authority with the power to enforce legal commands.

The anarchical character of the state system is emphasized by the "realist" or "neorealist" approach that goes back to Hobbes, who considered the fiction of the state of nature a reality at the level of international politics (*Leviathan*, chapter 13). While other (e.g., structural) approaches might account more effectively for certain aspects of contemporary international relations such as the increasing importance of transnational organizations and institutions, this realist perspective is, like the state-as-actor model, best suited for dealing with our main question: How relevant are moral judgments applied to *states* operating within the *present world order?*

The theory of international anarchy has been criticized as being incompatible with the fact that nations often cooperate for common purposes and comply with rules of international law and treaties. Thus, Stanley Hoffmann points out that states do not always seek "power after power," and "not at all times are states in a situation of war of all against all" (Hoffmann 1981, 14). The view that states are essentially contentious, which he attributes to Hobbes, is not even implied by Hobbes's own text. Hobbes says that governments are "in a state and *posture* of gladiators" (*Leviathan*, chapter 13; italics added). This situation does not exclude the possibility of voluntary cooperation between states, when it is in their common interest to cooperate. Indeed, "despite the absence of any ultimate international authority, governments often bind themselves to mutually advantageous courses of action" (Oye 1986, 1). Similarly, Charles Beitz claims that "it is wrong to conceptualize international relations as a Hobbesian state of nature" (Beitz 1979, 49), as if this view implied that "there are no reliable expectations of reciprocal compliance by actors with the rules of cooperation in the absence of a superior power capable of enforcing these rules" (Beitz 1979, 36). In the same vein, Keohane and Nye hold that "for political realists, international politics, like all other politics, is a struggle for power but, unlike domestic politics, a struggle dominated by organized violence" (Keohane & Nye 1977, 23).[1] Whether realists acknowledge the phenomenon of international cooperation, the model of international anarchy is perfectly compatible with the observations that "nations of the nuclear age are inescapably interdependent— dependent on each other's behavior" (Bundy 1984, 5), and that "security issues have diminished in salience relative to economic issues" (Hanrieder 1981, 137)—and, I might add, to common environmental concerns.

Nor does it matter whether it is true that the Hobbesian interpretation is "particularly weak in accounting for change, especially where the sources of that change lie in the world political economy or in the domestic structure of states" (Keohane 1986, 159), as long as this model provides a suitable interpretation of the international system in one particular historical period that includes our own. For the same reason, the following criticism seems not relevant here: "We no longer can afford the luxury of living by old-fashioned Hobbesian realism. The risks are morally unacceptable. Hobbesian realism as a framework for international relations must be modified, if we want to survive" (A. Cohen 1987, 233). Hobbesian realism is an empirical theory that explains—successfully, I believe—why certain states adopt certain foreign policies. To ensure survival in the nuclear age, the *facts* of international anarchy may have to be modified (by whom? how?—that is another question), not the *theory* that accounts for the present facts. Here I will be dealing only with moral judgments about foreign policies of states within the present system of a world divided into independent units, not with moral injunctions to modify the present situation (however desirable it may be, were it in anyone's power).

The theory of international anarchy has no moral or ideological implications, no more so than the state-as-actor model. It seems therefore unwarranted to speak of the "amoralism of realism" (A. Cohen 1987, 232) (unless by "amoral" is meant not "immoral," but "nonmoral") and to accuse realism of being conservative, "elitist and antidemocratic," "ethnocentric," of standing for "the rightful dominance of the Great Powers" (Rothstein 1981, 392, 395), and even of having "totalitarian implications" (Ashley 1986, 290). Robert O. Keohane, in spite of his criticism of realism, nevertheless concludes that "Realism is a necessary component in a coherent analysis of world politics because its focus on power, interests, and rationality is crucial to any understanding of the subject" (Keohane 1986, 159). It is precisely interests and rationality on which the rest of this chapter will focus.

2. Practical Impossibility and Practical Necessity

According to the instrumental view, criteria of rationality are applicable to the choice of means to given ends, but in general not to the choice of ends themselves. But I have already indicated that there are certain exceptions. For our topic, the most important exception is that it is not rational to select an end that is practically

unattainable. To best explain in what sense I will use the concepts of practical impossibility and practical necessity, I shall first give some simple examples. I will then apply these categories to foreign policy goals.

A prisoner whose cell door is securely locked cannot escape. Nor can he aim at escaping even though he could somehow break out of his cell if prison security is so tight that any attempt at escaping would be detected. That it is practically impossible for someone to adopt a certain goal means that this goal, while (strictly speaking) available, it is nevertheless "too *difficult*, or too *costly*, or too *painful*" (Goldman 1970, 209) to be pursued; too difficult or costly or painful, not just for this particular actor, but for any agent finding himself in the same situation (like that of the prisoner). This interpretation is in line with that given by several authors. "'Impossible' often means no more than 'prohibitively costly'" (Braybrooke & Lindblom 1963, 93). "In any concrete situation, only a limited number of alternatives are actually *feasible*; the other conceivable or *possible* alternatives are not available, typically because they would require more resources than exist" (Arrow 1982, 254). Similarly, "impossibility" in the legal sense has been defined as comprising "not only strict impossibility, but impracticality because of the extreme and unreasonable difficulty, expense, injury, or loss involved."[2]

A counterexample: John finds it too risky to attempt to save a drowning child. Yet it is possible for him to try to save the child. It is not the case that almost anyone in John's situation would find it too risky to try to save the child (in contradistinction to the prisoner's situation). Again, what matters is not the particular agent's inclination, but how anyone in the agent's position would typically act.

The situation of the prisoner can also be described in positive terms: it is practically necessary for him to remain in jail. Normally, "a person cannot help but adopt as a goal the avoidance of pain or hunger or suffering, other things being equal" (Raz 1978, 15), and to do so is practically unavoidable. Or take "primary goods" such as "income and wealth . . . , things which it is supposed a rational man wants whatever else he wants" (Rawls 1971, 92). Disregarding abnormal cases (e.g., ascetics or prisoners on hunger strike), individuals have practically no choice but to aim at least at securing a minimum of material well-being (which in turn is necessary to achieve any further end). One's life is perhaps the most important "primary good," and preserving it is a matter of practical necessity, disregarding exceptional circumstances such as risking one's life to save another's or committing suicide. Theoretically, a bank teller who is the victim of a holdup *could* risk his life for the sake of the bank, but practically he has no choice but to protect his life rather than the bank's funds, if these two goals conflict—as they do in the case of an armed robbery. If the menace is less credible, the teller may have an effective choice, as does John when he is confronted with the decision whether to attempt to save the drowning child. Accordingly, the expression, "It is practically necessary for an agent to adopt a certain goal" will be defined as "Anyone in the agent's position would normally find it too risky or difficult or costly to do otherwise."[3]

Practical necessity is not the same as expediency. An *expedient action* is one that is advantageous, or based on considerations of utility rather than of principle. To act expediently is to avoid any alternative conduct that is *more* difficult or more costly or more risky. Someone might find it expedient to cheat on his income tax (if he has reasons to believe that his fraud will not be detected), but to do so, while possible, is surely not practically necessary. Most everyone does not find it *too* costly to pay taxes, and most will pay fairly as a matter of principle.

It may be objected that categories such as "too difficult, too costly, too risky" and also "normally" are too vague to be applicable to concrete situations. How risky must a course of action be to be considered practically impossible? Admittedly, the borderline between feasible goals, on the one hand, and either practically ineligible or practically unavoidable goals, on the other, is fluid and depends on the situation under review. This, however, cannot be raised as an objection to the fruitfulness of the conceptual distinction between possibility and practical impossibility or necessity. Many social phenomena are continuous, and cannot be classified into neat either/or categories.

But are there not bank tellers who would or do risk their lives for the sake of the bank? It must be emphasized that, from the judgment that it is practically necessary for a certain person to adopt a certain goal, no inference can be drawn as to his actual behavior, at least not with certainty. The judgment that it is practically unavoidable for the bank teller to choose his life over the interests of the bank is true, even if he actually puts up resistance. It is true because almost anyone would, in a similar situation, find it too difficult to risk his life. Many people set themselves goals that are practically impossible for them to attain, and fail to do what is practically unavoidable.

Does not this make the concepts of practical necessity and impossibility a matter of mere convention? There is no way to avoid relativizing these notions with respect to the generally accepted preferences and values within a particular kind of culture, such as ours. One could imagine—but not without difficulty—a different society where resisting threats such as those facing the teller is the generally accepted norm. However, we are concerned here with our own society, and later with the international system as it functions in our historical period.

Does this approach amount to a celebration of selfishness? True, if not rescuing the child were the generally accepted norm, to do so would be practically impossible (but not therefore right). However, in most cultures, and certainly in our own (and even in New York City!) it is considered feasible to take at least some risk to help a person in danger. The proposed definition enables us to determine, at least in principle, whether adopting a certain goal is practically impossible, or practically necessary, or possible without being unavoidable.

Since the choice of ends cannot, in general, be qualified as rational or not rational, it is neither rational nor not rational for John to attempt to save the child or not to take any risk. On the other hand, it is rational for the bank clerk to give in to the gunman, because protecting his life is, under the circumstances, a practical necessity; trying to resist would be practically impossible, and therefore not rational. It is rational to aim at what is practically unavoidable, and not rational to attempt the impossible, either in a strict or in a practical sense, and regardless of what someone actually does.

3. The National Interest—A Practically Necessary Goal

In the absence of a supranational authority, national states find themselves in a situation similar to that of the bank teller facing the gunman when no immediate police protection is available. Both are in an anarchical situation, and both have no choice but to aim at their own self-preservation (individual or national) as a matter of practical necessity (but the way to realize that goal is, of course, quite different in the two different cases). Statesmen in their role of foreign policy–makers "have little choice but to put the interests of their own entity above those of others or of the international system" (Sondermann 1983, 58)—little choice in the sense of practically no choice but to act in their nation's self-interest—and to further the interest of other states or of supranational organizations only if compatible with their own national interest. Indeed, given the international system in which we have been living for many centuries, it is generally considered too risky for any statesman to adopt any foreign policy goal that is not compatible with his nation's self-interest. Consequently, it is rational for every government to aim at the protection of its nation's territorial integrity, military security, and economic welfare, and not rational to adopt foreign policy goals in conflict with its national interest.

Realists are often pictured, rather ambiguously, as holding that "the conduct of nations is, and should be guided exclusively by the amoral requirements of national interest" (M. Cohen 1984, 300). Realism, at least in the sense of adopting the model of international anarchy, does not entail either of these two views. The claim is not that the conduct of nations *is* in fact always guided by the national interest or that "states, the principal actors in world politics, *are* rational egoists" (George 1980, 3; emphasis added). Hans Morgenthau correctly states that "the foreign policies of all nations must necessarily refer to their survival as their minimum requirement"—"necessarily" in the sense of practical necessity. But he draws the incorrect conclusion: "Thus, all nations *do* what they cannot help but do: protect their physical, political, and cultural identity against encroachments by other nations" (Morgenthau 1952, 972). Nation-states cannot help but to do so only in the sense that it is practically necessary that they do, and that it is not rational for a government to pursue goals incompatible with the national interest. However, in accordance with the previous explication of the concept of practical necessity, the affirmation that it is practically unavoidable, and hence rational, for states to care foremost for their self-interest does not entail that they always do,

nor—as we shall see later—that they proceed rationally to implement the national interest even when they in fact have adopted this
necessary goal.

Nor does the thesis defended here maintain that the conduct of
nations "*should* be guided exclusively" by considerations of
national interest—not if "should" is taken in the moral sense (as I
shall emphasize in the next chapter). True, principles of rational
choice are normative, in the sense that they are, like moral principles, prescriptions for human conduct; but they prescribe what
agents should do to act, nor morally, but rationally. It is not the
purpose of this study to determine to what extent governments in
fact act rationally in this area, or to explain or predict specific
foreign policies on the basis of a "rationality assumption" (Keohane
1986, 165). The topic calls for specifying criteria that foreign policy
decisions must fulfill to qualify as rational, and determining
whether specific foreign policies satisfy these conditions. Answers to
these questions about rationality will have some bearing on the
problem of the relevance of morality to foreign affairs.

There is a further possible objection, based on game theory
considerations. The outcome of a state's foreign policy is affected
by, often unforeseen and unforeseeable, decisions of other states. In
such prisoner's dilemma situations, each of two agents is better off
by acting self-interestedly (whether the other agent acts self-interestedly or cooperatively), but it is still better for both to act in their
common interest. Take two states, A and B, who must decide
whether to "cooperate" (e.g., to conclude an arms reduction agreement and to abide by it), or to "defect" (e.g., to continue to arm).
If A increases its armaments relative to B, A is better off than if he
does not, especially if B also arms (the same is true for B); but if
both A and B agree to disarm, both are still better off than if they
do not and the race continues. Hence, "the pursuit of self-interest
by the means rationally recommended apparently turns out to be
self-defeating" (Barry & Hardin 1982, 378).[4] Does not this dem-
onstrate that rationality requires the subordination of self-interest
to the common good? Does not rationality require states to cooperate for the collective benefit of all nations rather than to pursue
their own national interest? It all depends on whether states A and
B trust each other. Acting self-interestedly is the rational strategy
for A if he does not trust B, and vice versa, as the armaments race

between the United States and Soviet Russia during the cold war period illustrates. Only if there was mutual trust between *A* and *B* would cooperation for their mutual benefit be the rational strategy.[5]

Thus, game theory does not show that it is always rational for a government to pursue the interest it has in common with other governments *instead* of its own interest. Game theory "demonstrates convincingly that the narrow pursuit of the national interest is frequently inconsistent with that very goal" (Chamberlin 1989, 276)—that is, with the national interest broadly conceived, and that it is sometimes rational to sacrifice the narrower to the broader national interest. In other words, the pursuit of a state's immediate national interest at the expense of another state's often makes both worse off, and it may therefore be rational to sacrifice short-term national interests to what is in the national interest in the long run. This consideration may well be incorporated into the very definition of the national interest: To pursue the national interest is to adopt policies furthering territorial integrity, military security, and economic well-being in the long run (even at the price of some immediate sacrifices in terms of these goals). Contrary to what Beitz declares, the Hobbesian position does not lead to the conclusion that "no state has an interest in following cooperative rules" (Beitz 1979, 63). That states have practically no choice but to aim at the promotion of their national interests is perfectly compatible with the recognition that a cooperative strategy is *sometimes* the rational way to achieve this necessary goal.[6]

A significant difference exists between domestic politics involving a great number of citizens and groups within a state, and international politics pertaining to relations between a relatively small number of states-as-actors. "Being cooperative in large number interactions to provide collective benefits typically is not rational" (Hardin 1985, 339) because it is often rational for an agent in a large group to be a free-rider (i.e., to benefit from a public good [from which he cannot be excluded] produced by others without sharing in the costs).[7] As Mancur Olson pointed out in his classical study: "If the members of a large group rationally seek to maximize their personal welfare, they will *not* act to advance their common or group objectives unless there is coercion to force them to do so" (Olson 1965, 2). Hence, as Hobbes already indicated, it is necessary to have a government with the authority to make it mandatory for a large group of citizens to cooperate in their common interest, by enacting and enforcing laws making it rational to do so rather than to incur sanctions against free riding. In the absence of a supranational authority, there is no such incentive for nations to comply with norms of international cooperation. However, "being cooperative in small numbers, especially dyadic relations, is commonly—but not always—rational in the narrow sense that it serves one's self-interest" (Hardin 1985, 339). Since the number of actors on the international scene is relatively small, states will often find it rational to secure their national self-interest by voluntarily adopting a cooperative strategy, even if such action involves relinquishing some elements of their sovereignty.

The decision of the twelve Western European countries to merge into the larger aggregation of the European Economic Community does not indicate that they have rejected the rational (because practically necessary) goal of the pursuit of their respective national interests for the sake of some different, supranational end. Rather, they realized that they would all be better off economically in the long run by relinquishing some of their sovereignty to the Community, and that it is therefore in the long-range national interest of each member state to act cooperatively rather than to pursue its immediate national interest or to defer to certain private interests that are bound to suffer, at least in the short run.

Given the anarchical structure of the state system, the national interest cannot rationally be traded off against foreign policy goals incompatible with this necessary end, but trade-offs can be made between the various elements of the national interest. As the previous example illustrates, it is sometimes rational for governments to balance one of the components of the national interest against some other component when they come into conflict—in this case to reduce national sovereignty for the sake of greater economic well-being. Even giving up national territory may serve the national interest. It was rational for France to relinquish its sovereignty over Algeria, not so much for moral reasons as for the sake of France's security; indeed, it would have been more rational to do so sooner than later, at the price of a needless war. Similarly, some Israelis argue that it is in Israel's national interest to "trade territory for peace," even if this policy should lead to an independent Palestinian state. A country under attack may consider it in its national interest to reduce the general standard of living of its population to increase military expenditures sufficiently to stave off the attack ("guns instead of butter").

4. The National Interest and Special Interests

While the national interest is a practically necessary goal for a state, and for the government acting on its behalf, individual citizens and groups have a choice whether to support governmental policies geared toward this goal.

In democratic systems, it will normally be in the self-interest of most citizens to favor national interest policies, as their own security and well-being are most often tied to those of the state. Even people under dictatorial rule are likely to have a stake in their country's security, especially when endangered. With the increasing probability of defeat, the Nazi authorities no longer needed to use ideological arguments to enlist the support of the German people; appeal to national survival was sufficient.

There are, however, ethnic, religious, and ideological movements openly hostile to the governments under which they happen to live, for example, Algerians when they were under French rule, blacks in South Africa, Palestinians in Israel, Kurds in several countries. Various Soviet republics tend to defend their ethnic interests, not only against each other, but also against the overall national interest of the Soviet Union. Given their values and goals, it may well be rational for such groups to oppose the national interest that it is rational for their governments to promote.

Government officials dealing with foreign affairs are in general also concerned with domestic politics. These dual concerns may confront them with a dilemma. In their role of foreign policy–makers, they are practically compelled to pursue the national interest. At the domestic level, governments have, like citizens, the choice between pursuing their own advantage, the advantage of some elite group to whom they are beholden, or the general public advantage; and within the latter category, they may have the option of choosing between various intrinsic goals such as enlarging freedom at the price of equality or vice versa, between favoring public welfare or private privilege, between legalizing or outlawing abortion, to give only a few examples.

For the purpose of maintaining or consolidating their own power within the state, government officials, like private citizens, tend to have a stake in the national interest. However, these two goals are sometimes in conflict. Then public officials are confronted with the choice of pursuing the national interest even at the peril of endangering their own position or of complying with the preferences of powerful groups advocating goals or policies detrimental to the national interest. It is not the case that "[T]he individual making a crucial decision (for example, the U.S. President) cannot act merely on the basis of his individual preferences for he is an agent, empowered to act only insofar as he does so in the nation's interest" (Bobbitt 1987, 110). He "cannot" act contrary to the national interest, only in the sense of practical impossibility, and only in his public role of agent empowered to make foreign policy decisions. As an individual, a statesman's primary purpose may be to stay in power; to achieve that end he sometimes acts deliberately against the national interest, in deference to the party or group on whose support his power depends. During the French Revolution Louis XVI allied himself with other absolute monarchs who invaded his own country to protect the aristocracy from the revolutionaries. After 1933, the British and French governments deferred to public opinion opposed to increasing armaments. Perhaps they misjudged the requirements of the national interest. More likely, they acted in this manner in order to maintain themselves in power, thereby endangering their countries' military security (foreseeably so, and foreseen by General De Gaulle). It is often claimed that United States policy toward Latin America has been traditionally geared to business interests rather than to national interests. Dictators, to consolidate their own power, often embark on foreign conquests even though these may put national security at risk; examples include Mussolini's invasion of Ethiopia, Nasser's attack on Israel, and Argentina's Falkland Islands venture.

Such instances have led some writers to draw the opposite conclusion: "Because demands frequently conflict, foreign policy tends to represent in any society, no matter what its political system, the demands of the most influential coalition of particular interests" (Knorr 1975, 32). This is not always the case either.

When such demands are not compatible with the national interest, it may be open to statesmen to resist these pressures. To refer to a previous example: During the Cuban missile crisis, President Kennedy did not submit to the demands of a large segment of the Republican party to adopt a more belligerent policy than would have been compatible with national security.

Thus, while it is rational for a statesman to pursue the national interest at the foreign policy level, it may at the same time be rational for him to subordinate the national interest to his goal of maintaining power domestically. Here we have a conflict between two intrinsic goals that cannot be resolved by the criterion of rational choice. It is a moral dilemma.

To summarize: I agree with realism "as a theory of self-interested choice by state actors interacting in a context of international anarchy" (Wendt & Duvall 1989, 51). This means not that state actors *do*, or *ought*, to act in the national interest, but that it is *rational*, because practically necessary, for actors in their role of foreign policy–makers to adopt the national interest as their intrinsic goal. To what extent can such decisions be considered morally right or wrong? We are now equipped to deal with this question.

Notes

1. Yet, Keohane does acknowledge that realists do not deny the possibility of international cooperation. "International regimes should not be interpreted as elements of a new international order 'beyond the nation state,' . . . [but] as arrangements motivated by self-interest: as components of systems in which sovereignty remains a constitutive principle" (Keohane 1984, 63).
2. American Law Institute, *Restatement of the Law of Contracts* (St. Paul, Minn.: West, 1932), para. 454.
3. While there are goals that are impossible to attain, both in a strict sense and in a practical sense, there are no strictly necessary goals. By definition, adopting a goal implies making a choice between that goal and an alternative one (e.g., not choosing that goal). It is strictly impossible for the prisoner to open the cell door in order to escape; but remaining in his cell, while strictly necessary, is not a goal, since he has no other choice.
4. "Each player is better off personally by playing the selfish strategy *no* matter what the other does, but both are better off if both choose the unselfish rather than the selfish strategy" (Sen 1977, 340). Consequently, "if each

rather than neither does what is certain to be better for himself, this will be worse for both of them" (Parfit 1986, 59).

5. I am borrowing from Anatol Rapoport's distinction between individual and collective rationality: "*individual* rationality . . ., prescribes to each player the course of action most advantageous to him under the circumstances, and *collective* rationality . . ., prescribes a course of action to both players simultaneously. It turns out that, if both act in accordance with collective rationality, then *each* player is better off than he would have been had each acted in accordance with individual rationality" (Rapoport 1982, 72).

6. "Intergovernmental cooperation takes place when the policies actually followed by one government are regarded by its partners as facilitating realization of *their own objectives*" (Keohane 1984, 51).

7. "Each person may have an incentive to induce others to cooperate and to defect from the joint strategy in the hope of enjoying the fruits of cooperation without incurring the costs of compliance" (Coleman & Ferejohn 1986, 6).

3
Morality and Foreign Policy Goals

T he primary function of speech acts propounding moral principles or expressing moral judgments is to guide the conduct of
those to whom they are addressed.[1] Bestowing moral praise or
blame also aims at influencing agents to persevere in their behavior
or to modify their conduct. In the era of international politics,
moral utterances are found in the writings of moral philosophers,
political scientists, and journalists. Such speech acts sometimes urge
citizens to support or to oppose certain foreign policies (of their
own government or of other countries). Typically, moralists address
themselves to foreign policy decision makers and aim at influencing
them to enact, or not to enact, certain foreign policies on moral
grounds. Moreover, declarations by politicians often include moral
arguments to justify their foreign policies.

In this chapter I shall deal with what I consider to be one of the
two foremost issues of morality in foreign policy: When is it
relevant to exhort government to adopt certain foreign policy goals
for moral reasons, and when are such recommendations pointless?
Here the distinction between the national interest and other ends is
pertinent. The next chapter examines the range of relevance of
ethics to the choice of specific policies implementing chosen foreign
policy goals—the other main issue.

1. Morality and Practical Necessity

To clarify the problem of the relevance of ethics to foreign affairs,
we need to examine the adage "'ought' implies 'can.'"According to
this maxim, "*A* ought to do *X*" implies that "*A* can do *X*," and "*A*
can do *X*" in turn implies that there is at least one alternative

action, *Y*, that *A* can perform *instead* of *X*; that is, it is possible for *A* not to do *X*. Acting implies having a choice: walking is an action; falling is not. If "ought" implies "can," the contrapositive also holds: if *A* cannot do *X*, it is not the case that *A* ought to do *X*; nor is it the case that *A* ought not to do *X*, given that he has no choice but to abstain from doing *X*.

That "ought" logically implies "can" has been denied, and rightly so. If "*A* ought to do *X*" logically entailed "*A* can do *X*," then Bill, who incurred a debt he cannot now repay, would not be morally required to repay it. "If 'ought' entailed 'can,' an agent could escape having to do something by making himself unable to do it" (Sinnott-Armstrong 1984, 252). Yet it is not contradictory to hold that Bill ought to repay his debt even though he cannot do so.

To subscribe to the maxim "'ought' implies 'can,'" we must give the term "implies" a different interpretation. We are not dealing with an implication in the sense of logical entailment, but with a pragmatic sort of implication.[2] Keeping in mind the action-guiding function of moral speech acts, my saying to *A* that he ought to do *X* is *relevant as advice* only if *A* can do *X*. "The principle that 'ought' implies 'can' springs from this guiding aspect of norms. Subjects can be guided by their awareness of a norm to do only what it is possible for them to do" (Darwall 1983, 203). If *A* cannot do *X*, my propounding that *A* nevertheless ought to do *X* is not logically false, but it is pointless as advice. "One cannot speak 'prescriptively' and also ask the impossible" (White 1975, 151). Similarly, if *A* cannot help but do *X*, it is irrelevant to urge him on moral grounds either to do *X* or to refuse to do *X*. "The inevitable and the impossible must be taken as given. What lies in between constitutes the appropriate scope for choice" (Goodin 1982, 127)—and for ethics.

It seems to me that these considerations are applicable, not only to strict but also to practical necessity and practical impossibility. To make this clear, I shall return to some of my previous simple examples. Their simplicity will make it easier to deal with the relevance of ethics to foreign policy goals. Let us go back to the bank clerk who theoretically could resist, but practically cannot risk his life to save the bank some money. It would be pointless to advise him that he nevertheless has a moral duty to protect the bank (or, for that matter, to remind him that he has a moral right to protect his own life). "There is no point in asking the 'ought' question when the practical question does not arise" (Hare 1963, 53). By contrast, John's dilemma whether to try to save a drowning child raises a genuine moral issue, and providing moral advice in his case would be pertinent. I pointed out earlier that it is *rational* to do what is practically inevitable, and *not rational* to attempt to do what is practically impossible. I now must add that it is *pointless* to call either action right or wrong, because in neither case are there alternative actions that are practically feasible. "According to [the 'ought' implies 'can'] principle, people are not morally required to do what they lack the power to do or what involves so great a sacrifice that it would be *unreasonable* to ask them to perform such an action" (Sterba 1987, 132; italics added). Conversely, choices between available goals, while nonrational, can be subject to moral appraisal. Right and wrong must pertain to what is effectively possible.

It might be objected that to "guide conduct" is a function of judgments of rationality as well as of morality. Yes, but there is a difference. If I caution someone, advising him that it would not be rational for him to adopt a certain goal because it would be practically impossible for him to reach it, my advice would be pertinent. I hope thereby to dissuade him from attempting what is not feasible. But once he realizes this impossibility, there is no point in urging him *on moral grounds* to refrain from pursuing that goal. Similarly, if a goal is a practically necessary one, its rationality is a sufficient reason for adopting it, and the argument that it is morally right to do so is redundant. Judgments of rationality are applicable, not only to possible actions (they may be rational or not), but also to practically necessary and impossible conduct (the former is rational, the latter not). To fall within the purview of ethics, actions must be practically possible (neither practically necessary nor practically impossible). Only when the agent has a practical choice is it relevant to advise him what he ought to do on moral grounds.

2. Morality and the National Interest

We can now pull the threads together to arrive at one of the main conclusions of this study.

1. States are actors on the stage of world politics.

2. In the absence of a supranational authority, it is practically unavoidable for any state to care foremost for its own national interest (as previously defined), and it is therefore rational for statesmen to pursue their state's national interest.

3. Propounding moral principles is relevant when the agent is faced with possible choices, but it is pointless to qualify the adoption of a practically necessary or a practically unavailable goal as either right or wrong.

Given these premises, the conclusion is inescapable. The national interest being a practically unavoidable goal for any state, it is pointless to advise statesmen that the pursuit of the national interest is either moral or immoral. As Machiavelli pointed out in his *Florentine Histories*, "Things done out of necessity must not and cannot merit praise or blame."[3] Or, as our contemporary George Kennan has written:

> These needs [the object of the national interest] have no moral quality. They arise from the very existence of the national state in question and from the status of national sovereignty it enjoys. They are the *unavoidable necessities* of a national existence and therefore not subject to classification as either "good" or "bad." (Kennan 1985, 206; italics added)

To urge governments to pursue the national interest *on moral grounds* is to engage in a redundancy. To advise statesmen to pursue a goal incompatible with the national interest is to dissuade them from acting rationally. True, "the concept of conduct applies to the behavior of states." But it is not true that "no conduct is in principle exempt from moral assessment" (Holmes 1989, 97–98). The conduct of states is not susceptible of moral assessment, as far as such conduct consists of the pursuit of the national interest.

We must note a significant difference between foreign and domestic politics. There are hardly any domestic policies that governments are practically compelled to pursue. They are confronted with choices between various, often competing goals—for example, with the problem of how to balance freedom of speech with national security, or economic freedom with collective welfare, or the interests of management against those of labor or consumers. Such trade-offs do involve moral conflicts.

At the foreign policy level, too, statesmen are sometimes faced with moral choices. Contrary to what some followers of the realist school argue, the thesis that the national interest is a practically necessary goal does not imply that "moral categories are simply out of place in the realm of international affairs" (M. Cohen 1984, 299). Moral considerations are relevant whenever statesmen must decide whether to adopt a goal different from, but compatible with, the national interest.

3. When Moral Judgments Are Not Relevant

Pursuing the National Interest Considered Moral

That it is rational to pursue the national interest is a sufficient reason for doing so, and to qualify it as morally right is redundant. This thesis contrasts with the following statement:

> The national interest is a compelling constraint only because governments accept a pattern of values in which national security and prosperity enjoy high priority. So, for an individual statesman the problem is . . . how to balance the claims made upon him by conflicting moral principles. (Garnett 1984, 90)

For the individual statesman, national security and prosperity is not a moral principle, to be balanced against other moral values. The national interest is a "compelling constraint" because it is a practically unavoidable goal that cannot reasonably be traded off with conflicting foreign policy goals. The same objection applies to Hans Morgenthau's statement that "the state has no right to let its moral disapprobation . . . get in the way of successful political action, itself inspired by the *moral principle* of national survival" (Morgenthau 1973, 10; italics added). To aim at securing national survival is not a moral principle, but a practical necessity for the state. For the same reason, it is incorrect to qualify the Hobbesian theory as propounding "the necessity (or '*duty*') to follow the national interest" (Beitz 1979, 28; italics added). It cannot be both.

The former characterization is the correct one. It is a necessity—perhaps an unfortunate necessity. Indeed, this approach does not involve any reverence for the present system of independent states, nor any defense of patriotism, let alone of nationalism. It may well be deplorable that our world happens to be carved up, in many instances quite arbitrarily, into sovereign entities, as this division tends to foster a feeling of national superiority on the part of citizens everywhere.

A government's moral obligation to pursue the national interest has also been derived from its moral duty to promote its citizens' well-being insofar as this well-being is intertwined with the security of the state. This argument would be applicable to liberal democracies, but not to regimes with authoritarian ideologies. But even democratic systems might appeal to a different norm, namely, that the government's foreign policy should reflect majority opinion even if such opinion favors goals incompatible with the national interest.

But is not the pursuit of the national interest praiseworthy when it is in turn a means for the pursuit of our own moral ideals? Do we not praise the United States and Great Britain for having entered the Second World War to fight for the "four freedoms"? But they had practically no choice but to fight for their national security (and England and the Soviet Union for their very survival). The Second World War produced a fortunate coincidence between political necessity and moral principle. We may be pleased when governments standing for our own values act rationally in the area of foreign politics, and deplore it when they do not. Governments can be praised on moral grounds for their democratic institutions and practices, but not for protecting their national security, whatever their regime.

Even if the pursuit of the national interest were a moral requirement, this would be an ambiguous norm. Does it bestow on every nation the right or duty to protect their respective national security? If so, which nation's interest ought to prevail in case of conflict? Is the victor morally entitled to "take all"? Do ethnic groups have the right to form their own nations in opposition to the interests of their present governments? Or does the alleged right depend, as Michael Walzer would have it, on "the moral standing of any particular state," which in turn "depends upon the reality of the common life it protects" (Walzer 1977, 54), that is, upon whether its people are "governed in accordance with its own traditions" (Walzer 1980, 212)?[4] Such a formulation hardly enables us to determine whether a given state is, or is not, entitled to pursue its national interest. Or, as nationalists are prone to argue, does the alleged moral principle of national interest pertain only to one's own nation because of certain characteristics it alone possesses ("My country, right or wrong!")? The United States, because it is the "leader of the free world"? Iran, because it crusaded (under Khomeini) for the true faith against the infidels? There is no "moral community of mankind" that could serve as the basis for the resolution of such issues; there are deep cleavages of moral outlook from state to state (e.g., between advanced and underdeveloped countries), not to speak of radically different moral systems held by different groups even within a single state. Nor do I need to get involved in such ethical controversies, since all states must pursue their national interest out of practical necessity, not out of moral choice.

Pursuing the National Interest Considered Immoral

I mentioned earlier (chapter 1, Morality) that egoism tends to be considered immoral in our ethical tradition. Accordingly, it would be wrong for a state to be guided by its national interest, at least if this national interest conflicts with international or supranational injunctions. But I have also indicated that egoism, too, can be and has been considered morally right, and I have just examined critically the view that the pursuit of the national interest is a moral duty.

"Morality" has even been *defined* as excluding egoism. Baier, for example, says:

> By 'the moral point of view' we *mean* a point of view which furnishes a court of arbitration for conflicts of interest. Hence it cannot (logically) be identical with the point of view of self-interest. Hence, egoism is not the point of view of morality. (Baier 1958, 189–190)[5]

If egoism is, by definition, not a moral principle, morality must consist of rules "for the good of everyone alike" (Baier 1958, 200).

Applied to international relations, it follows that "what is in the national interest is one thing, what is morally right is another" (Lackey 1984, 2). Now, definitions are linguistic stipulations, and as such neither true nor false, but more or less fruitful in a given context. Defining *morality* as excluding egoism in general and as excluding the pursuit of the national interest in particular is using this term to apply only to the speaker's own moral point of view. It would then be *logically* false to say that acting in one's self-interest or in one's national interest is moral. Even merely *using* this definition would not *prove* that egoism is wrong, and that states should subordinate their national interests to the good of all nations alike. Substantive ethical norms are not derivable from definitional stipulations, just as they cannot be deduced from factual premises alone.[6]

There is another argument to prove that cooperation for the common good is morally right and that egoism is immoral: "If all pursued dictates of morality [in this sense] rather than rationally pursuing their own self-interests, all would be better off" (Sen 1982, 77). Applied to international relations, this thesis could be restated as: All states are better off if they cooperate to achieve common purposes than if they pursue their own narrow national interests. This argument supposedly proves that states ought to act "morally." However, the prisoner's dilemma illustrates (see chapter 2) that it is not rational for agents to cooperate for their mutual benefit unless each can be fairly certain that the other(s) will contribute his/their share(s). "We would all be better off if we could trust each other through our shared sense that moral requirements *are* overriding reasons for acting" (Darwall 1983, 181). But can governments trust one another? That is the crucial question. If there is mistrust, as there was between the United States and the Soviet Union during the cold war period, noncooperation is the "dominant strategy." If there is mutual trust, cooperation may be rational, and may coincidentally also be considered moral. Mutual trust among the major powers did prevail at the moment of Iraq's invasion of Kuwait. This accounts for their collective action through the mechanism of the United Nations, which promoted their common interests, especially the national interests of the oil-consuming nations.

Whether reciprocal confidence is warranted is often a matter of disagreement. Some Israelis, mistrusting Palestinians specifically and Arabs generally, argue that acting "morally" endangers Israel's very survival. Fanatics among them bolster their opposition to any agreement by appealing to a different ethical norm, arguing that Israel's right to exist takes moral priority over Palestinian demands. Other Israelis are more optimistic, and hold that granting Palestinians in the occupied territories autonomy or even independence is more likely to ensure Israel's security than having to cope with continued Palestinian hostility. That this policy is morally right is at most an additional consideration.

Democratic societies tend to identify morality in foreign policy not only with cooperation for common purposes, but also with upholding the tenets of liberal democracy.

> There are no special geopolitical clients, no geopolitical enemies other than those judged to be such by liberal principles. Therefore, the United States, as a liberal state, must have no liberal enemies and no unconditional alliances with non-liberal states. This policy . . . requires *abandoning the national interest* and the balance of power as guidelines of policy. (Doyle 1987, 203; italics added)

True, it is often in the national interest of the United States to support liberalism abroad. But when these two goals conflict, it would not be rational, rather than not moral, to abandon the former as a guideline for United States policy. For example, the United States had to keep Spain as a "geopolitical client" even under Franco, Greece as a client even during the rule of the Colonels, the Philippines under Marcos, and Iraq under Saddam Hussein during its war with Iran (although this decision might be questioned in the light of subsequent events). This is not to deny that the United States has often supported nonliberal regimes even when it was against its own interest to do so, which illustrates again that governments often fail to act rationally in foreign affairs. Or take the following generalization: "Looked at from a moral point of view, it cannot be right for one nation to allow the people of another nation to become the hostages, captives, slaves or victims of its own government" (Bedau 1979, 42). If the United States were to comply with this moral point of view, it would have to attempt the rescue of every population whose basic rights are violated by their respective governments. In many cases this would be an ineligible goal, which could be pursued, if at all, only by the use of military force. It is clearly out of the question for the United States to try to prevent the violation of human rights in North Korea, Iran, Iraq, or Cuba—to give only a few examples.

Sometimes government itself enacts principles that it cannot implement, and sometimes it explicitly acknowledges such impossibility. Thus, section 502B of the Foreign Assistance Act of 1961, as amended, stipulates that

> a principal goal of the foreign policy of the United States shall be to promote the increased observance of internationally recognized human rights by all countries. . . . Assistance may not be provided . . . to a country the government of which engages in a consistent pattern of gross violations of internationally recognized human rights.

Yet the same section does allow economic and military aid to human rights violators if "on all the facts it is in the national interest of the United States to provide such assistance." This latter clause has been criticized on the grounds that "we may not justifiably pass up opportunities to protect and promote the rights of the citizens of other nations simply because it is in the national interest to do so" (Brown 1979, 167). The author implicitly acknowledges that these two goals may conflict. When they do, efforts at protecting human rights abroad would be politically mistaken. It may thus be rational, from the point of view of the national interest, to provide military aid to countries that violate human rights, or to maintain military bases in such countries, as, for example, in South Korea, moral arguments to the contrary notwithstanding.

Without explicitly claiming that it is wrong to pursue the national interest, governments often find it expedient to present this goal in the guise of high moral principles. For example, an American strategic planning document of the cold war period states that "our free society, confronted by a threat to its basic values, naturally will take such action, including the use of military force, as may be required to protect those values" (quoted by Postbrief 1981, 685). This document makes the implicit claim that the

United States will use its military forces in an unselfish, hence "moral," way for the defense of its "values," not selfishly, hence immorally, to protect its national security. Did the authors of this document realize that it would in most cases be contrary to the national interest to use military force for the sole purpose of "frustrating the Kremlin design" and of protecting people against "the evil men who have enslaved them"? Or did they use such emotive language to elicit domestic support for possible policies of over-commitment?

American presidents have been prone to use such moralizing rhetoric, which George Kennan has characterized as the "histrionics of moralism" (Kennan 1985, 212). I shall give two illustrations, from the beginning and the end of the cold war.

On 12 March 1947 President Truman requested Congress to provide military and economic assistance to Greece and Turkey—a policy that soon became known as the Truman Doctrine:

> I believe that it must be the policy of the United States to support free peoples who are resisting attempted subjugation by armed minorities or by outside pressures. I believe that we must assist free peoples to work out their destinies in their own way. (Vital Speeches of the Day, 15 March 1947, 322–324)

If this were in fact a guiding principle of American foreign policy, its government would have intervened in Czechoslovakia in 1939 against Nazi Germany and in 1948 and in 1968 against Soviet Russia, to mention only two of countless cases, but such actions would have been incompatible with maintaining America's national security.[7] It was, however, in its national interest to provide aid to Greece and Turkey (and to other European countries the following year under the Marshall Plan). The president acknowledged, but only incidentally, that "the national interest of this country [is] involved."

The end of the cold war brings us to the "Reagan Doctrine." I am not here concerned with whether the policy of aid to the Contras against the government of Nicaragua was good policy or bad policy. I am only concerned with the way the president attempted to justify his policy:

> Our mission is to defend freedom and democracy. . . . We must
> not break faith with those who are risking their lives—on every
> continent, from Afghanistan to Nicaragua—to defy Soviet-
> sponsored aggression to secure rights which have been ours from
> birth. (State of the Union Address, February 1985, quoted by
> Luper-Foy 1988, 183)

The alleged goal was not so much the protection of American
security against alleged Soviet aggression, as the championing of
"freedom and democracy" against "Marxism-Leninism." The
implication is that great power rivalries are really confrontations
between rival ideologies, and a regime stands for "freedom and
democracy" if—and only if—the administration considers support
in its national interest.

Now I will turn to a more recent example. When President Bush
ordered U.S. air and ground forces into Saudi Arabia after Iraq's
invasion of Kuwait, his stated purpose was "to stand up for what's
right and condemn what's wrong all in the cause of peace," and "to
assist the Saudi Arabian Government in the defense of its homeland." Only incidentally did the President mention that "our country now imports nearly half of the oil it consumes and could face a
major threat to its economic independence" (*New York Times*, 9
August 1990), and he did not spell out his goal of preventing Iraq
from gaining control over nearly half of the world's oil production.
In a similar vein, Secretary of State James Baker, in his meeting with
President Assad in Damascus, characterized America's involvement
in the Gulf as follows: "Our policy cannot and never will be
amoral. We can have close relations only with countries that share
our fundamental values" (*New York Times*, 16 September 1990).
This generalization is refuted by America's actual foreign policy in
this very instance, where its national interest required it to have
close relations with regimes not sharing its fundamental values.
"Moral advice not to submit to the necessities of survival . . . would
be advice to commit national suicide" (Wolfers 1962, 59)—at least
in some situations.

4. When Moral Judgments Are Relevant

"If the statesman . . . must be selfish for the state's survival, security, and interests, can one really talk about morality at all?"

(Hoffman 1981, 40). The claim that moral judgments concerning national interest are pointless because statesmen have no choice ("must," in this sense) but to aim at their state's survival does not entail skepticism about all morality. Moral directives are appropriate *whenever agents have eligible choices.* As mentioned before, individuals, in their private lives, do in most circumstances have options to act egoistically or altruistically or in the interest of some larger group or for some common cause. They are free to decide to obey or to disobey the law, and their defiance may be judged wrong or right. Soldiers may be held morally obligated to disobey orders rather than to commit war crimes. Whatever the official policy on foreign aid, individuals have the option of contributing to relief, foreign or domestic. Citizens may have moral reasons either to support or to oppose their government's policies or to promote the interest of a regime their own government opposes. Government itself usually has choices in the domestic sphere, as mentioned before. We have also seen that a statesman's necessary goal of pursuing the national interest may come into conflict with his *possible* goal of staying in power. Most important to the topic, "international conduct is open to moral assessment" (M. Cohen 1984, 302), but only when it does not involve the national interest.

Here are some examples of foreign policy goals that can be meaningfully appraised from a moral point of view.

Promoting Human Rights

Whether *individuals* should contribute to the advancement of human rights worldwide (e.g., by joining Amnesty International) is clearly a moral question. But should governments pursue this goal? It has been held that, "since human rights is a goal additional to the national interest, pursuing such a policy would seem inevitably to involve sacrificing the national interest one way or another" (Fairbanks, Jr. 1982, 87). Not inevitably so. We have seen that "to promote the increased observance of internationally recognized human rights by *all* countries" or "to defend freedom and democracy" as a worldwide mission would indeed "involve sacrificing the national interest," assuming that such endeavors were not utopian. But to champion these values in *specific* countries is a possible goal, for the United States, for example, and compatible with its national interest. Take the question whether the United States should

influence the South African government to end apartheid, perhaps
by means of economic sanctions or divestment. It may be that pursuing this goal is neither detrimental to nor conducive to America's
national interest, and that not doing so also has no effect on the
national interest. Indeed, American investment represents only a
small fraction of the total foreign investment in South Africa. "The
United States, in sum, has no vital interest in South Africa"
(Ambrose 1988, 291). Here, it makes good sense to favor America's
promotion of human rights in South Africa on moral grounds.

Unlike the United States, the British government felt that it
could ill afford economic sanctions against South Africa because of
its traditionally strong economic ties with that country. This
pragmatic argument was not, however, the argument used by
Prime Minister Thatcher to defend Great Britain's policy. Perhaps
to avoid the appearance of cynicism, she took the moral offensive
and accused the *advocates* of sanctions of immorality. Their policy,
she argued, would lead to "starvation, poverty, and unemploy-
ment" among black South Africans. "That to me is *immoral*. I find
it repugnant. . . . When people call that moral, I just gasp."[8] That
this reasoning is specious[9] is not our concern here. The point is
that Mrs. Thatcher apparently did not dare to openly express her
conviction that sanctions against South Africa are detrimental, not
merely to British business interests, but to the national interest
itself; otherwise she would not have found it expedient to present
herself as a vestal virgin.

When the U.S. House of Representatives voted to set up a program to promote democracy in Poland and Hungary (*New York
Times,* 20 October 1989), it made a moral decision, but such aid
was no doubt consistent with, if not actually conducive to, America's
national interest. Take a counterexample: It has been questioned
whether President Carter's human rights policy was compatible
with America's national interest. Some have argued that it was not,
at least not as far as it was directed at the Soviet Union, because it
impaired the chances of détente. If so, adopting the human rights
goal was not rational in this instance, moral considerations to the
contrary notwithstanding. Someone might say in defense of Carter's
position: "Never mind the national interest; human rights are more
important," without realizing that he recommends doing what is
not rational with respect to what is practically necessary. He might

argue instead: "It is not a matter of choice between two alternatives: human rights *or* national interest. Both goals can be made compatible, if we are willing to pay a small price in terms of national interest for a great gain to an important cause." Here I must reply that it is not rational to trade off even a small loss in terms of a practically necessary goal against a great material or moral gain with respect to some alternative but incompatible end. (Such trade-offs are possible when it comes to the choice between foreign policies by which to pursue the national interest, as will be pointed out in the next chapter.) It is then left to the defender of Carter's approach to claim that his support of Soviet dissidents at that time did not endanger détente in the least; or he could even argue that promoting human rights in the Soviet Union, like supporting democracy in Poland, in turn promoted America's national interest. We see here that the question as to whether ethics is relevant in this area often depends on questions—often controversial—of fact.

Should the United States refrain from exporting arms to governments that violate their citizens' basic rights? This is certainly another controversial issue. Some might argue that this policy does not interfere with the national interest. Others might point out that not exporting weapons causes the loss of potential customers to foreign competitors who do not have such moral scruples. Here we encounter again the difficulty mentioned earlier. Using the concept of the national interest commits us to the assumption that it can, at least in theory, be objectively ascertained. Yet politicians and commentators often disagree as to whether the adoption of a certain goal such as the promotion of human rights is conducive to or detrimental to the national interest, or just compatible with this necessary goal. If conducive, to adopt it is rational, and if detrimental, it is not rational. The same applies to the policy of bolstering regimes that violate human rights. Moral considerations are not relevant in any of these four possible situations. On the other hand, if the national interest is not affected one way or another, it is pertinent to urge the government to contribute to the propagation of basic rights and other democratic values *on moral grounds*, and to blame the government for acting contrary to these principles. However, this raises another ethical question: Does the United States have the moral right to foster its "way of life" on different societies, and to act as a global moral policeman?

Global Distributive Justice

Norms of distributive justice stipulate how benefits and burdens should be allocated among agents. Distributive justice at the international level concerns such questions as: How shall the burdens of cooperation for mutually beneficial public goods be divided among *states* (e.g., their financial contributions to international institutions like the United Nations, or to efforts to prevent a further deterioration of the world environment)? Such rules must restrain states from free-riding (e.g., from benefiting from cleaner air without contributing their fair share). Another problem of distributive justice, and the one I want to deal with here, is the extent to which relatively well-off nations are morally obliged to contribute to the relief of poverty in underdeveloped countries. The question is not whether a *person's* moral duty to relieve distress extends to those beyond the border of his own country, but whether there are such obligations of transfer between rich and poor *states*, as a matter, not of charity, but of justice. Third world nations argue that they have a claim on a more egalitarian allocation of wealth and resources against industrialized countries because they are the victims of past colonial and neocolonial exploitation. Advanced states are thus confronted with the question of to what extent, if any, they are obliged to narrow the gap.

Lately, there has been some discussion as to whether Rawls's theory of justice,[10] and more particularly his difference principle, is applicable to welfare transfers from rich to poor countries.[11] Briefly, Rawls considers principles of redistribution just if they would be agreed to by rational, self-interested persons in a hypothetical "original position," that is, "behind a veil of ignorance" in which "no one knows his place in society, his class position or social status; nor does he know his fortune in the distribution of natural assets and abilities, his intelligence and strength, and the like" (Rawls 1971, 137). Rawls claims that such agents would unanimously choose the "difference principle" that stipulates that "social and economic inequalities are to be arranged so that they are . . . to the greatest benefit of the least-advantaged" (83).[12]

Rawls does propose to extend the fiction of the original position to "justice between states" (378), and to think of persons participating in this worldwide social contract "as representatives of different nations who must choose together the fundamental principles to adjudicate conflicting claims among states" (378). They are assumed to "know nothing about the particular circumstances of their own society, its power and strength in comparison with other nations" (378). Nor do they know whether they are representatives of a rich or poor country. But Rawls does not deal explicitly with the possible application of the difference principle to the redistribution of wealth between nations. Such an extension would lead to the requirement that inequalities of wealth be arranged in such a way as to make the worst-off countries as well off as possible (Barry 1989, 188).

Whatever one's assessment of Rawls's theory of justice, for our purpose it suffices to acknowledge a moral attitude in advanced societies deploring the wide (and perhaps widening) gap in the living standard between themselves and the third world (as well as between individuals within the same country), and advocating a fairer distribution of resources worldwide somewhat along the lines of Rawls's difference principle. Governments of wealthy countries are thus faced with the problem of how to reconcile the demands of global distributive justice with the national interest.

At one extreme we have the case of emergency relief to countries stricken by natural disasters or by tribal warfare. The cost to wealthy nations is so small (especially relative to the great benefit to the receiving countries) that they do not really affect their national interest. Here, moral exhortation is clearly relevant. The other extreme would be to apply to wealthy states the norm propounded by Peter Singer to individuals:

> that we ought to give until we reach the level of marginal utility—that is, the level at which, by giving more, I would cause as much suffering to myself or my dependents as I would relieve by my gift. This would mean, of course, that one would reduce oneself to very near the material circumstances of a Bengali refugee. (P. Singer 1979, 33)

At the international level, this would result in an equally low standard of living worldwide, an equalization going much further than Rawls's difference principle which does allow *inequalities* in distribution beneficial to the least advantaged countries. Since the

national interest of a wealthy nation includes maintaining its existing level of economic well-being with its relatively high average
living standard, such equalization is clearly out of the question.
Somewhere between these extremes one could, in theory, find the
point up to which national interest and global justice are compatible. Even by this criterion, there is no doubt that the redistribution called for "is very much larger than the current level of transfers, and also a good deal more for all relatively wealthy countries
than the one percent of gross national product that is the most
given in aid by any country now" (Barry 1986, 78). Moral exhortation to wealthy countries to increase foreign aid is clearly fitting.

Norms of distributive justice are principles of deontological
ethics (see chapter 1, Morality). There are also consequential arguments in favor of economic aid to third world countries. Just as it
is sometimes in the interest of democratic states to promote the
protection of human rights by other countries, "to make the worst-
off countries as well off as possible" does in turn further the economic interest of advanced societies, as they have a stake in a
healthy world economy. Here, too, utilitarian considerations of
national interest are perhaps of greater weight than appeal to
deontological ethics. If France or Sweden gives, in terms of their
GNP, more foreign aid than does the United States, this may indicate not so much that their governments have a higher moral sense,
but that they have more foresight with respect to their long-range
national interest.

Another example: The twenty-four leading industrial nations
decided (in Brussels on 4 July 1990) to grant economic aid to other
countries on the basis, not of purely economic criteria (as does the
World Bank and the IMF), but of the following norms: "Adherence
to the rule of law, respect for human rights, the introduction of
multiparty political systems, the holding of fair and free elections,
and the development of market oriented economies" (*New York
Times*, 5 July 1990, A–1).[13] These are moral goals (except the last),
which may be recommended either as being compatible with the
national interest of the advanced nations or on the grounds that
encouraging other countries to protect their citizens' human rights
will, in the long run, further the national interest of the providing
states.

Imperialism

Imperialism may be defined as a state's endeavor to conquer and dominate other states beyond the requirements of its own national security. It is "expansion for the sake of expanding, . . . dominion for the sake of ruling" (Schumpeter 1951, 5). According to our moral standards, while promoting human rights or providing foreign aid is laudable, imperialism is evil.

Yet imperialism, too, is sometimes compatible with the national interest, as were Napoleon's and Hitler's goals of domination over most of Europe, until both made the—from their point of view—fatal mistake of deciding to conquer Russia. Their earlier conquests were surely not required to safeguard national security, and are therefore morally condemnable. Their invasions of Russia, on the other hand, are to be criticized for having been based on miscalculation, and moral considerations are secondary, if not irrelevant. Other recent examples include Argentina's attempt to extend its sovereignty over the Falkland Islands and Soviet Russia's endeavor to conquer Afghanistan. To generalize: Imperialistic ventures, if they succeed, are immoral, and if they (foreseeably) fail, unreasonable.

Governments tend to rationalize imperialistic endeavors, no less so than the pursuit of the national interest, as unselfish sacrifice for some cause, such as freedom or justice. To quote Chateaubriand, "Justice is so sacred, and seems so necessary to the success of one's undertakings, that even those who batter justice claim to act only to abide by its principles."[14] It is not surprising that Saddam Hussein justified his imperialist conquest of Kuwait on moral grounds. Like President Bush, he did not stress the material aspects of the situation; both resorted to moralizing rhetoric, using almost identical words. "This is a war of right against wrong," the Iraqi leader declared on 5 September 1990, but continued, appealing to a morality quite different from President Bush's, "and is a crisis between Allah's teachings and the devil. . . . It is now your turn, Arabs, to save humanity from the unjust powers who are corrupt and exploit us" (*New York Times*, 6 September 1990, A–19).

For the victims of imperialism, national independence, instead of being a practically necessary goal, may have become (at least in the short run) an impractical one. Then different goals may become possible without being necessary, and therefore subject to moral judgment. One option may be to save lives and to capitulate without a fight, as Denmark did in World War II; another may be to uphold the *idea* of national continuity and to go on fighting against all odds, as did Poland.

Should imperialism be forcefully opposed by countries other than its victims? Wording it this way, the question is not well put. Preventing or repelling or punishing imperialist conquest, like imperialism itself, is a goal that may be either detrimental to, or compatible with, the necessary pursuit of the national interest. In many cases, it is contrary to a state's national interest to come to the aid of a victim of imperialist attack by counterattacking the aggressor state. Urging such a state to do so on moral grounds would then be recommending a course of action that fails to be rational. It also happens that a government, by adopting the goal of anti-imperialism, furthers its own national interest. In such cases, an appeal to morality is redundant. Moral considerations are relevant only if, from the point of view of a country's national interest, it does not matter whether it embarks on an anti-imperialist course of action. There are few situations of this kind. Military intervention tends to be risky and costly, and therefore rational only if it is, from the point of view of the national interest, the lesser evil in comparison with leaving imperialism unchallenged. In either case, moral considerations are beside the point.

To recapitulate: It is not relevant to judge the pursuit of the national interest right or wrong, since it is practically unavoidable, and hence rational, for states to adopt this goal. It is only by coincidence that the pursuit of the national interest sometimes leads to outcomes judged morally desirable. Claiming to be guided by moral principles when pursuing the national interest is often counterproductive. Adopting, on moral grounds, a foreign policy goal detrimental to the national interest is not rational. Morality has its place when it comes to the choice of foreign policy goals other than promoting the national interest, but consistent with it. "There are [moral] constraints on the way a government can conduct its foreign policy. This simply means that a government is not allowed to do whatever it wants, disregarding the effect of its actions on people outside its borders" (MacLean 1979, 96). There are moral constraints on a government's foreign policy goals *other than, but compatible with, its national interest.*

To recapitulate this chapter schematically:

	The national interest	Goals	
		Compatible with the national interest	Incompatible with the national interest
Recommending it as moral	redundant	pertinent	not rational
Opposing it as immoral	not rational	pertinent	redundant

Notes

1. See Hare 1963, 10.
2. *Pragmatics* considers the use of symbols, such as the expressive function of speech acts. *Syntax* deals with the logical relations between symbols, and *semantics* with their meaning.
3. ". . . delle cose fatte per necessitá non se ne debbe ne puote loda o biasimo meritare" (chapter 11).
4. Similarly, Charles Beitz argues that "only states whose institutions satisfy appropriate principles of justice can legitimately demand to be respected as autonomous sources of ends" (Beitz 1979, 81).
5. See also Harman's statement, chapter 1, section 4, Morality.
6. Both are fallacious arguments; the former is known as the "definist fallacy," the latter as the "naturalistic fallacy," of which the former is a special case (see Frankena 1973, 96–102).
7. General Marshall later recalled that, as secretary of state at that time, "my facilities for giving [the Russians] hell . . . was 1 1/3 divisions over the entire United States. That is quite a proposition when you deal with somebody with over 260 and you have 1 1/3" (quoted by Ambrose 1988, 79).
8. *Guardian*, 9 July 1986, quoted by Lukes 1986, 179.
9. As Lukes points out, "a principled refusal to engage in certain consequential calculations, to dirty one's hands by doing harm that would credit a Christian idealist or a dedicated Ghandian, ill suits the Iron Lady, Victor of Inflation and the Falklands" (Lukes 1986, 183).
10. John Rawls, *A Theory of Justice*, is perhaps the most widely discussed book among political philosophers since its publication in 1971.
11. See Barry 1986, 1989.
12. This is part of Rawls's second principle of justice. Its underlying idea is that, "while the distribution of wealth and income need not be equal, it must be to

everyone's advantage" (61). Rawls's first principle (which does not concern us here) stipulates that "each person is to have an equal right to the most extensive basic liberty compatible with a similar liberty for others" (60).

13. Romania was excluded by virtue of these criteria.

14. "La justice est si sacrée, elle semble si nécessaire au succ`es des affaires, que ceux mêmes qui la foulent aux pieds prétendent n'agir que d'apr`es ses principles" (Chateaubriand, *Mémoires d'outre-tombe*, book 20, chapter 13).

4
Rationality, Morality, and Specific Foreign Policies

W hat is the place of morality when it comes to specific foreign policies aimed at the pursuit of the national interest? Here, too, the answer depends on whether there are alternative policies that also meet the criterion of rationality.

While the pursuit of the national interest itself is rational because practically necessary, there is some doubt as to whether the criteria are applicable at all to foreign policies aimed at the national interest. Theoretically, a foreign policy–maker must, to act rationally, survey all alternative policies available to him in a given situation, assess the probability of their effectiveness with respect to his national interest goal, and determine their side effects and further consequences. Some political scientists have concluded that "there is no science of foreign affairs that can assign probabilities and values to possible outcomes of alternative courses of action" (Kipnis 1987, 108), especially in view of the fact that the outcome of a state's foreign policy decision is also affected by the—often unforeseen—decisions of other states. It is true that foreign policy decisions must generally be made under conditions of uncertainty rather than of risk, the probabilities and utilities not being quantifiable.[1] Yet, "when the situation is recognized as one of uncertainty, rational choice theory is limited, but not powerless" (Elster 1989, 11). For instance, one might apply the maximin rule that requires us only to consider the worst possible outcome of each action and "to adopt the alternative the worst outcome of which is superior to the worst outcome of the others" (Rawls 1971, 152)—in other words, to choose the lesser evil.[2] It is important for governments to apply the canons of rational choice to their foreign policy decisions as best as possible, as "departure from the rational choice model imperils the survival of the state" (Waltz 1954, 201)—at least in certain situations. As I mentioned when I defined the concept of the national interest, for the purpose of the topic I must assume, in spite of all the difficulties, that there are objective criteria by which to determine whether a given foreign policy does promote this necessary goal.

It has also been argued that, because of the trend toward bureaucratization in modern societies, there is a "decreased relevance of rationality models for understanding policy and [an] increased importance of the bureaucratic model" (Morse 1981, 152), especially for an understanding of foreign policy. "The nature of the bureaucratic political process seems to contradict almost the very notion of our government even pretending to make coherent, purposive foreign policy" (Destler 1981, 167). Granted that bureaucratic rivalries and compromises increase the danger of unreasonableness of the resulting foreign policies, this situation actually increases the importance of determining to what extent, if any, these policies measure up to the requirements of the rationality model.

1. When Moral Judgments Are Redundant

Unlike the national interest *goal*, the *means* of securing it is never a matter of practical necessity. Sometimes one strategy is clearly so much more preferable to all other possibilities that we are inclined to consider its adoption indispensable. We say that the United States had no choice but to go to war against Japan after the attack on Pearl Harbor. However, "no choice" is here a figurative way of speaking. Declaring war was not practically unavoidable. Even in this extreme situation, the United States had other options, for example, merely to threaten retaliation, or to try to arrive at some solution by diplomatic means. That "war was the only choice" means here no more than that this was no doubt the most appropriate course of action under the circumstances, and that any other policy would have been detrimental to the national interest.

A single policy that is clearly the most suitable with respect to the national interest is to be recommended as rational, just like the national interest goal itself, and acting otherwise must be condemned as failure to act rationally. To endorse the former policy as morally right or to criticize the latter as immoral is redundant.

Rational Policies Considered Moral

Morality is the best policy—sometimes. This does not mean: Choose the morally desirable foreign policy because it will often turn out to be the best way to promote the national interest. It does mean: Choose the most effective policy; it often happens that the most effective policy corresponds to our moral convictions. It should be adopted because it is rational to do so, not because it meets with our moral approval. Its rationality is not only a necessary but also a sufficient condition for endorsing it, and there is no need to appeal to morality in addition.

A goal can be valued both intrinsically, for its own sake, and extrinsically, as a means to a further end. We have seen that propagating democratic values, furthering economic development of poorer countries, or improving the environment worldwide may be endorsed morally as goals compatible with the national interest of the advanced democracies. These measures may also be judged desirable not only in themselves, but also because they promote the national interest of the contributing nations—a much stronger argument. A previous example fits here: America's initiative (through the United Nations Security Council) to mount economic sanctions against Iraq and a multinational military presence in Saudi Arabia to counter the invasion of Kuwait. Was there a coincidence between two different, but compatible goals: standing up for the moral principle not to allow reaping benefits from unprovoked aggression and promoting the national interest? Or was morality merely a window dressing for the pursuit of the national interest as it was perceived by the government of the United States? The last seems the most plausible interpretation, as one may well wonder whether the same measures would have been taken if there were no oil under the sands.

It is clearly in the long-range interest of many states to comply with international law, to participate in international organizations, to conclude commercial treaties and disarmament agreements. Here again, rationality, not morality, is the determining factor. It has been said that "governments are morally obliged to support international institutions that produce public goods from which they, and inter-national society as a whole, benefit" (Keohane 1989, 116). If a government derives benefits from supporting such institutions, appeal to moral obligation is superfluous. Another example: The nations that drew up the Hague Convention of 1907 foresaw the possibility of their becoming involved in wars. "And, presumably in the light of calculated national self-interest and the principles of common humanity, they decided which rules they were prepared to commit themselves to follow" (Brandt 1974, 32). Whatever their actual motives, the first reason is sufficient for adopting such rules, and moral principles "of common humanity" hardly count.

This last example brings up the question, Is the "moral" policy really the "best" policy? As mentioned earlier (chapter 3, When Moral Judgments Are Not Relevant), and as the prisoner's dilemma indicates, this may depend on whether states can trust one another. If mutual trust is lacking, "morality" and rationality point in differ-ent directions, and it will be rational to pursue the national interest in an uncooperative way.

Conversely, pursuing the unavoidable goal of promoting the national interest may in turn further the moral end of upholding democratic values. To take a previous example: The Allies had to go to war against Germany and Japan for the sake of their national security and even their very survival. This necessary, nonmoral goal in turn contributed to the morally desirable end of upholding the "four freedoms." The latter may be considered a moral fringe bene-fit, so to speak, of a rational course of action.

Policies Lacking Rationality Considered Immoral

Immoral policies are sometimes not rational. Just as rationality is the best argument for endorsing a foreign policy if it is the only adequate, or clearly the most successful, one available, not being rational is a sufficient reason for opposing it, and to condemn it as immoral is, again, redundant.

A country likely to be attacked by another must take prepara-tory measures to withstand the coming blow. Great Britain and France failed to do so after 1933, despite ample evidence and explicit warnings concerning Hitler's design. Their lack of prep-aration has often been condemned as lack of moral fiber. True perhaps, but the decisive reproach is surely that their failure to rearm was a failure to act rationally in terms of their national security, leading to their capitulation at Munich in 1938.

If it is true, as it has been claimed, that the American government (and specifically the CIA) gave money to keep down the Communist vote in Italy as late as 1985, this policy is to be condemned, not so much as an immoral interference with the free electoral process of a European ally, but as a mistaken policy, based on the erroneous assumption that the Italian Communist party has remained an instrument of Soviet policy when it had in fact become a conservative movement, in the sense of standing for the democratic status quo.

During the Vietnam War opinion was sharply divided between those who extolled the venture as a moral crusade against "world communism"[3] and those who condemned it as immoral. Both views seem to me mistaken. Assuming that the administration was really out to defend freedom (in South Vietnam!) against communism, it should have been criticized for having chosen a "moral" goal incompatible with the national interest. The antiwar movement should have blamed the administration, not for having made an immoral decision, but for using military force for the pursuit of a goal incompatible with national security. According to a third view, the government did indeed have national security in mind,[4] believing that it would be endangered by the communization of Indochina (the domino theory). As we know with hindsight, and as was foreseeable (and foreseen by some), this was a case of overextension detrimental to national security (and would have been so even if we had "won"). The policy should therefore have been condemned as not rational rather than as immoral, and Talleyrand's dictum might be applicable: It's worse than a crime, it's a mistake (C'est pis qu'un crime, c'est une erreur). (It is the way the war was fought that is open to moral scrutiny, as I shall point out.) In a similar situation, the Soviet foreign minister acknowledged that Soviet Russia's attempt to conquer Afghanistan was immoral as well as mistaken.[5] From the Soviet point of view, the second consideration should have been sufficient to dissuade its government from embarking on this venture.

As mentioned before, the United States may well have acted contrary to its national interest, at least in the long run, by bombing Libya, mining Nicaragua's harbors (and refusing to accept international jurisdiction), invading Grenada and Panama. If so, the lack of rationality of these policies is a sufficient reason for opposing them, and moral condemnation is superfluous.

A Justice Department memorandum of 21 June 1989 authorizes the president to order the seizure of fugitives in foreign countries without the host government's consent. This measure was defended by referring to court rulings allowing the president to "depart from international law on behalf of the national interest" (*New York Times*, 9 November 1989). Our first impulse might be to claim that it is immoral to violate international law even if doing so serves the national interest. However, the decisive consideration is "that our legal position may be seized upon by other nations to engage in irresponsible conduct against our interest" (*New York Times*, 9 November 1989).[6]

2. When Moral Judgments Are Counterproductive

Rational Policies Considered Immoral

If the policy under consideration is the only effective way to protect the national interest, then to condemn that policy as immoral is, at least implicitly, to come out for a policy that fails to be effective, and hence to be rational.

England's and France's appeasement of Nazi Germany at Munich in 1938 has been called "shameful" (Hoffman 1981, 61). While it was mistaken—and perhaps shameful—for England and France not to have increased their armaments as soon as Hitler came into power, capitulating to Hitler at Munich was the only thing Chamberlain and Daladier could reasonably do, even though selling out Czechoslovakia was incompatible with the moral duty to fulfill treaty obligations and to come to the aid of a victim of totalitarian aggression. To criticize the Munich agreement as immoral is to recommend the only alternative: engaging Germany's superior military power at a moment when it would not have been rational to do so.

Could not one consider British and French appeasement at Munich wrong but "excusable" (Walzer 1974, 91) because to resist Germany at that moment would have been too risky to be a legitimate moral stance? To offer excuses is an implicit admission of wrongdoing. To pursue a practically necessary goal such as the national interest by the only suitable means is not wrong (or right), but rational (although sometimes deplorable). "It is possible even for a means which is itself bad to be outweighed and therefore 'justified' by a sufficiently good end" (Mackie 1977, 159), and the practically necessary end of the national interest always justifies—not morally but rationally—the only effective means, even though it often violates our moral convictions if considered in isolation; for example, if it requires the use of military force. That it is sometimes rational to act contrary to our moral feelings in foreign affairs is to be accounted for, not by an alleged depravity of "human nature," or by a supposed innate "aggressive instinct," but by the structure of our international system. This is not to deny that evil men sometimes wield political power, or to affirm that rationality always takes precedence over morality. If the goal is immoral, like imperialist expansion, so are the means, even if they are rational in terms of that goal.

Policies Lacking Rationality Considered Moral

Being guided by moral principles in the area of foreign politics easily leads to advocating or adopting measures that are not rational. America's involvement in Vietnam has been justified, as well as criticized, on moral grounds, as I mentioned. President Carter's human rights policy comes to mind again. If the Truman and Reagan doctrines were taken literally and actually carried out, they would lead to disastrous policies of overcommitment. Yet, according to Stanley Hoffman, "aid to a victim of armed external aggression" is "unambiguously" a legitimate justification for non-defensive war (Hoffman 1981, 61). As I indicated, acting in conformity with this principle at Munich would not have been rational, and moral rightness would have been no valid reason for confronting Hitler at that time.

Or take the war between Iran and Iraq. As is evident, at least after the facts, going to war was contrary to the interest of either country, as both suffered immense economic and military losses, not to speak of wasted human lives. Whatever the actual motives of each government, both claimed to have been driven by morality—different moralities.[7]

One may well wonder whether the American government acted in the national interest when it changed its assignment to its armed forces in the Gulf from defending Saudi Arabia against a possible Iraqi attack to forcing Iraq out of Kuwait, invoking the moral principle that aggression should not be rewarded, but punished.

3. When Moral Judgments Are Relevant

Choice between Several Effective Foreign Policies

So far, we have been dealing with situations where a single policy is clearly the most effective one available. However, in most circumstances foreign policy–makers are faced with the choice between various strategies, none of them *a priori* decidedly superior to all others. There is often uncertainty as to which is the most effective, or there may be agreement that several courses of action are more or less equally conducive to the national interest. This is where moral considerations are relevant, just as they are when there is a choice of a goal compatible with the national interest (See chapter 3, When Moral Judgments Are Not Relevant).

For example, American governments have been criticized for having gone further in their relations with Franco, Marcos, Noriega, or the shah of Iran than was required for the sake of military security, and that it was not necessary "to make love in public with the Greek Colonels" (as a foreign diplomat pointed out to me). Using restraint would have served the national interest just as well (if not better). If so, moral considerations are in place. Or take America's response to China's violent suppression of human rights in June 1989. The administration had the choice of issuing mild reprimands combined with mild and temporary economic sanctions (and sending the national security adviser to China soon after these events) or of reacting more decisively and more punitively. If both alternatives were equally compatible with America's national interest, it was to the point to reprove the administration for having chosen the former option. Similarly, if a state can influence another state's foreign policy just as effectively either by diplomatic means or by military intervention, it is pertinent to invoke the moral principle that armed force should be used only when peaceful means are of no avail.

The question often remains whether two policies under consideration can be reasonably expected to be equally effective. Those who criticize a policy as immoral have the burden of demonstrating that an alternative policy without the moral defect would have been as effective—a thesis that defenders of the policy are likely to dispute. Critics of America's bombing of Libya, mining of Nicaragua's harbors, and invasions of Grenada and Panama argue that refraining from these military measures would have served the national interest just as well, and that the immorality of these actions should have tipped the scales. Defenders of the administration hold that national security required these operations. "Prohibiting the U.S. Government from engaging in morally unacceptable activities" (MacLean 1979, 97) is relevant when alternative, morally acceptable policies are at least as effective.

Let us now suppose that there is a choice between a highly effective policy and another that is also adequate, but slightly less so than the former. Suppose also that the first policy is highly immoral, and the second morally right, or at least not wrong. Is it rationally warranted to trade off a very small loss in national interest terms against a great moral gain? There is general agreement that dropping atomic bombs on Hiroshima and Nagasaki was a sufficient condition for bringing about Japan's capitulation. Defenders of these actions claim that it was also a necessary one, that is, that Japan would otherwise not have given up, at least not so quickly as after these events. Some of President Truman's advisers argued that Japan could also be induced to capitulate by dropping an atomic bomb on an uninhabited island as a warning. However,

> when their proposals were judged unlikely to end the war as quickly as direct military use, they could not fall back on a claim that there was a moral or political imperative against killing civilians in a new and terrible way. Even the doubters were in some measure prisoners of the overriding objective of early victory. (Bundy 1988, 96)

Should the doubters have persisted, and argued that the greater probability of an earlier victory ought to have been overridden by the moral duty not to cause innumerable innocent victims?[8]

We have seen that it is not rational to trade off a loss, however small, in terms of the practically necessary goal of the national interest against a gain, however great, with respect to some other, incompatible foreign policy goal. But since foreign policies adopted in view of the national interest are never practically necessary, the range of rationality may well be extended to include the "second best" policy. Rationality is then compatible with the injunction not to pursue the national interest in the most effective, but highly immoral, way when a slightly less effective policy is available without the moral defect. The end does not justify the means, in the sense that it is not morally permissible to pursue a very desirable or a practically necessary end by the most effective means, *provided* there are alternative ways to reach it that are morally right (or less wrong), even if somewhat less adequate. Accordingly, it would have been reasonable for President Truman's advisers to recommend paying the price of a somewhat longer road to victory for the sake of avoiding the infliction of great harm. Advocates of the bombing of the two cities evidently felt that the alternative strategy involved a greater than the minimum risk to national security affordable for the sake of morality. Here we have a genuine moral dilemma.

We previously considered relief of world poverty as an application of the moral principle of distributive justice compatible with the national interest of the contributing nations, provided such aid does not involve a lowering of their own living standards. But if furthering the development of the underdeveloped countries is in turn conducive to the national interest of the developed states, it may be rational for the latter to make the sacrifice of a *slight* lowering of their own collective well-being. There is then a choice to be made between two morally desirable policies (not, as in the case of Hiroshima, between an immoral strategy and avoiding doing wrong), where one (giving more) is morally superior to the other. Here, again, it makes sense to urge advanced countries to opt for what is, in national interest terms, the "second best" policy, because it is morally superior at a relatively small material sacrifice.

Shortly before Iraq's invasion of Kuwait, the Senate and House voted to cut off U.S. loan guarantees to the Baghdad government that it had used to purchase American commodities, mainly farm products. The Bush administration had opposed rescinding these loans, arguing that to do so would not only harm American farmers, but also worsen the country's trade deficit. Senator Kassebaum defended this measure as follows: "I can't believe any farmer in this nation would want to send his products, under subsidized sales, to a country that has used chemical weapons and a country that has tortured and executed its children" (*New York Times,* 27 July 1990). Congress evidently felt that this was a small price to pay in terms of the national interest for the sake of upholding an important moral principle—a very small price, as the House voted "to allow the Secretary of Agriculture to waive the sanctions if he determined they cause more harm to American farmers than they do to the Hussein Government" (*New York Times,* 27 July 1990).

It might be objected that this approach lets in a great deal of morality through the back door, so to speak. Not if the criteria of a rational foreign policy are relaxed to include only strategies *almost* as effective as the best one available, and *greatly* superior from a moral point of view.

Still, this leaves several questions unanswered. How can one decide whether the "second best" policy is "slightly" less effective than the very best (and still rational), or greatly inferior, or even detrimental to the national interest? How can one measure or even estimate the degree of moral worth to be sought or moral damage to be avoided? How can one compare a loss of effectiveness with a gain of moral worth? Needless to say, the principle advanced here provides only some guidelines, of possible help when the stakes are high in terms both of morality and the national interest.

Choice between Expediency and Truthfulness

Government officials operating on both the foreign and domestic levels are often faced with different kinds of moral conflict. I mentioned the dilemma between a statesman's pursuit of the national interest and his concern for his own power that may require the adoption of foreign policies incompatible with that necessary goal.

Democratic governments are often confronted with the following moral choice. To get their proposed foreign policy enacted, they need the approval of the legislature and, hence, of public opinion-at-large. Democratic principles impose on democratic leaders the duty to be truthful and not to deceive the people. But people, and especially the American people, are inclined to view foreign policy as a contest between righteousness and the forces of evil. Therefore, the most expedient way for government to win public endorsement of its national interest policy is often to "sell" it in idealistic guise. As we have seen, this is the tactic the American government has been using consistently. Take President Truman's request to Congress for aid to Greece and Turkey in 1946, evidently a matter of American national interest. To rally Congress "to shell out tax dollars to support the King of Greece, Truman had to describe the Greek situation in universal terms, good versus evil" (Ambrose 1988, 85), that is, to equate "free peoples" with people living under anti-Communist governments of whatever type. As a result of this rhetoric, "the American people rallied behind their leader in a cause that transcended national, economic, social, and military interests: the cause of freedom itself" (Ambrose 1988, 86). Characterizing the Contras as "freedom fighters" against the "evil empire" or the invasion of Panama as "Operation Just Cause" served the same purpose, to enlist public support for foreign policies the administration considered—correctly or mistakenly—to serve the national interest. Army indoctrination should be mentioned in this connection.[9]

I criticized this line of argument by pointing out that, if it were taken at face value, it would lead to policies detrimental rather than conducive to the national interest. But perhaps we should approve of such misinformation, at least if it paves the way for the enactment of reasonable foreign policies. Here we have a genuine moral dilemma—between expediency and truthfulness.

However, while such moralizing rhetoric sometimes achieves its purpose for internal consumption, foreign governments and people whose support may also be needed are less likely to be taken in, and more inclined to unmask virtuous postures as mere propaganda and to denounce it as hypocrisy. There is also the danger that government officials become prisoners of their own ideological pronouncements. To avoid being accused of inconsistency or insincerity, they may feel compelled to "stick to their principles," even if this leads to foreign policies detrimental to the national interest.

To recapitulate this chapter schematically: With respect to the national interest, the policy under consideration is

	Effective		*Ineffective*
	The Only One	*One of Several*	
Recommending it as moral	redundant	pertinent	not rational
Opposing it as immoral	not rational	pertinent	redundant

Notes

1. "Risk is defined as a situation in which numerical probabilities can be attached to the various possible outcomes of each course of action, uncertainty as a situation in which this is not possible" (Elster 1986, 5).
2. We will see later (in chapter 6) how the maximin rule has been applied to the question of the morality of nuclear deterrence.
3. "History and our achievements have thrust upon us the principal responsibility for protection of freedom on earth," President Johnson proclaimed in 1965 in connection with the Vietnam War (quoted by Schlesinger 1986, 16). "The primary motive . . . had little to do with national interest at all. It was, rather, a precise consequence of the belief that moral principles should govern decisions of foreign policy. It was the insistence of seeing the civil war in Vietnam as above all a moral issue that led us to construe political questions in ethical terms" (Schlesinger 1971, 72).
4. "We felt our national interest required it," President Johnson's speech of 27 July 1965 (quoted by Schlesinger 1986, 76).
5. In the words of the Soviet foreign minister: "We went against general human values. We committed the most serious violations of . . . civilian norms" (*New York Times*, 24 October 1989).
6. To the objection that seizing people without the host countries' permission would "lend support to the Governments of Iran, Panama and Nicaragua to do the same thing," the assistant attorney general responded: "I reject any notion of moral equivalency between the United States and outlaw countries" (*New York Times*, 9 November 1989)—a wrong appeal, to wrong morality.
7. "We should try to export our revolution to the world" (Khomeini in a speech of 24 March 1980). "We cannot maintain the nation's honor by defending Iraqui territory only; our duty extends to every part of the Arab homeland" (Saddam Hussein in a speech of 8 February 1979) (both cited by Sick 1989, 120).

8. I am here disregarding the argument of defenders of the actual policy that prolonging the war would have caused even more deaths, both American and Japanese.
9. For example: "In a ready expression of what could be described as a central tenet of popular American ideology, American troops [deployed in Saudi Arabia] will often say that they are here to defend freedom or liberate the underdog, Kuwait, from the bully, Iraq. 'The United States has been the one in history that is first to help and do what it says it will do. . . . You know, the land of the free!' " (*New York Times*, 30 September 1990, A–20). According to this report, "We're here to protect our supply of oil" was heard less frequently.

5
Morality and War

W hen it comes to war and peace, moral feelings tend to run high, and moral principles are readily invoked. What is their relevance?

Moral philosophy follows the traditional legal distinction between norms stipulating under what conditions resort to war is prohibited or permitted or required (*ius ad bellum*), and rules determining what kinds of military actions are legitimate or illicit once war has broken out (*ius in bello*).

1. Resort to War

Contemporary ethical theories on just and unjust wars are reflected in various legal rules adopted by the United Nations. On 11 December 1946 the General Assembly adopted the Charter of the Nuremberg Military Tribunal, which considers as "crimes against peace" the "planning, preparation, initiation or waging of a war of aggression." The Charter of the United Nations stipulates that "all members shall refrain in their international relations from the threat or use of force against the territorial integrity or political independence of any state" (Article 2[4]), but reaffirms "the inherent right of individual or collective self-defense if an armed attack occurs against a Member of the United Nations" (Article 51). The following definition of the key word, "aggression," was adopted by the United Nations General Assembly on 14 December 1974: "Aggression is the use of armed force against the sovereignty, territorial integrity or political independence of another State."

According to the doctrine underlying these stipulations, states, like persons, are autonomous and sovereign; they must be considered legitimate at the international level, regardless of whether they treat their own citizens as autonomous persons. Translating these legal rules into moral terms, a war of self-defense against aggression is the only instance of a just war. Every other kind of warfare is a war of aggression and as such unjust.

Michael Walzer, in his widely discussed *Just and Unjust Wars* (Walzer 1977),[1] still puts the emphasis on the immorality of warfare and on the legitimacy of all states at the international level, even if they violate their citizens' basic rights. But he does enlarge the sphere of permissible military intervention, if only slightly. State *A* is morally entitled to go to war against state *B*, not only to defend itself against an attack by *B*, but also under certain other, clearly specified conditions, for example, "whenever a government is engaged in massacre or enslavement of its own citizens or subjects" (Walzer 1980, 217).[2] According to Walzer, "Humanitarian intervention is justified when it is a response (with reasonable expectations of success) to acts 'that shock the moral conscience of mankind'" (Walzer 1977, 107). But *A* has no right to attack *B* if *B* is engaged only in "ordinary oppression" of its citizens (Walzer 1980, 218).

The test of *im*permissible military intervention is the degree of "fit" between the government's domestic policies in the area of human rights and the opinions about these matters prevalent in the "community," that is, "the degree to which the government actually represents the political life of its people" (Walzer 1980, 214)—in other words, whether the populace is "governed in accordance with its own traditions" (Walzer 1980, 212). There may therefore be a fit between government and community in nonliberal-democratic regimes (Walzer 1980, 216).[3] Such states, while lacking domestic legitimacy, are still legitimate at the international level and therefore have the right *not* to be attacked by other states. The people's right to revolt against "ordinary oppression" by their own government does not confer a right of military intervention on other states, unless there is an absence of fit between government and community values, as is presumably the case if the government engages in the massacre or enslavement of its own people.

Several authors have extended the range of just war beyond Walzer's limit. David Luban justifies military intervention against states violating human rights amounting only to ordinary oppression. Contrary to Walzer, and contrary to the provisions of the United Nations Charter as well, Luban argues that "an aggressive war . . . intended to defend socially basic human rights" may be just, and "a war of self-defense . . . in order to preserve the status quo which subverts human rights" unjust (Luban 1980, 176). According to Luban, the bearers of rights of sovereignty are not states (the United Nations's view) nor communities (Walzer's approach, reminiscent of Edmund Burke), but individuals. A state governing without the consent of the governed is illegitimate externally as well as internally, and "cannot derive sovereign rights against aggression from the rights of its own oppressed citizens, when it itself is denying them those same rights" (Luban 1980, 169).[4] Gerald Doppelt, too, criticizes "the conservative dimension of Walzer's commitment to de facto governments as the cornerstone of international morality" (Doppelt 1978, 21), even when domestic revolution is justified.

Stanley Hoffmann advocates extending "legitimate causes of nondefensive wars" to certain "ends that transcend the (evident) interest of the initiating state" (Hoffmann 1981, 61). If state *A* has been attacked by state *B*, it is not only *A*'s government that has the right to counterattack *B* (by virtue of its right to self-defense); a third country, *C*, may justifiably intervene on *A*'s side to uphold the principle of collective security, one of the "world order ends" (61). But it is morally wrong to intervene "by force against a legitimate revolutionary movement abroad," as the United States did "in Iran in 1953, in Guatemala in 1954, at the Bay of Pigs in 1961" and against Allende in Chile and Ortega in Nicaragua (72).

Do the principles formulated by Walzer and by his critics enable us to ascertain whether a specific instance of waging war is right or wrong? It seems to me that the concepts used are too vague to make such determinations possible. Was Germany's remilitarization of the Rhineland in 1934 an act of aggression? Does self-defense include defense of "an absolutely vital security interest" (Hoffmann 1981, 59) like the Suez Canal or the Panama Canal? Aggressive wars are generally claimed to be defensive. Does a preemptive strike launched against an imminent attack constitute self-defense or aggression? (Israel's strike against Egypt in 1967 comes to mind.) "Legitimacy" and the terms used to define it raise many questions. Where is the limit between "ordinary oppression" and "massacre and enslavement"? How does one judge whether a regime is based on "consent of the governed" or fulfills "conditions of justice"? Applying Walzer's criterion of "fit" leads to rather paradoxical consequences. No doubt there was a close fit between the Nazi regime and the prevailing views of the German "community" (and the measures taken by the Nazis did not "shock the conscience of mankind" until much later). But there was not much of a fit between the Fascist regime and the Italian people's tradition and culture. If this was true, allied warfare was justified as "humanitarian intervention" against Italy, but not against Germany; the war against Germany could only be justified as a war of self-defense. Or suppose a government practices massacre and enslavement of its citizens *in conformity with* the political tradition of its people (examples are not hard to find). Walzer's principles would both permit and prohibit military intervention.

Moreover, states faced with the momentous decision whether to wage defensive or offensive war are not likely to be influenced by such moral injunctions. A government contemplating an attack will not change its mind because the target state has an internally legitimate regime (judged by whatever criteria). Nor will the attacked country strike back if, and only if, it has the moral right of self-defense (again, by whatever standard). Conversely, a government not inclined to war is unlikely to reverse its decision because its potential enemy oppresses its citizens (in an ordinary way or to an extreme degree). Governments are unlikely to be concerned with criteria of "just and unjust wars" or of "duties beyond borders," whatever they may be, and moral advice to go to war or to refrain from taking up arms usually falls on deaf ears.

This brings us back to our main question: Is it relevant to advise statesmen that resort to war is morally prohibited or permitted or required? For an answer, the main conclusions here are applicable.

Suppose that going to war is clearly the most effective, or perhaps the only, way to protect a state's territorial integrity. The rationality of the decision is a sufficient reason for endorsing it. It is beside the point to appeal to the *moral* right of self-defense or the *moral* duty of humanitarian intervention, except for propaganda purposes. It is just as pointless to warn a government that it is about to embark on an unjust war of aggression against a legitimate regime.

In our era war has become increasingly risky and costly, and resort to arms has therefore become more likely to be contrary to the national interest. This being the case, there is no need to invoke the immorality of war. To urge the government to take up arms nevertheless because of its moral duty to deliver a community from tyranny is to recommend a policy lacking rationality, and possibly to invite disaster. Curiously, Hoffmann's justification of non-defensive war for ends that transcend the national interest such as aiding the victim of aggression resembles the Truman and Reagan doctrines, and could be invoked to justify armed intervention Hoffmann himself would almost certainly oppose. It is true that realists are inclined to oppose military intervention.

> Thus the traditional realist position ends almost ironically: beginning with a dismissal of the relevance of ethical concerns to the issue of intervention, realists end up offering an implicit (or at least easily inferred) normative argument against interventionist foreign policy on grounds of prudence and moderation. (Smith 1989, 9)

There is no inconsistency here. That interventionist foreign policy is (often) imprudent is a *normative* argument, but not a *moral* one; it refers to rationality, not to rightness.

Even so, ethics does have a place in the crucial area of war and peace. Imperialistic expansion is sometimes compatible with national security (as I have indicated). Here, government has a choice, and it is relevant to condemn such military ventures as violation of the *moral* principle that war is wrong except if indispensable for the protection of national security.

The same moral principle can be invoked to condemn military intervention if the national interest can be secured as effectively by diplomatic as by military measures. Critics of the U.S. invasion of Panama argued that this action, while perhaps compatible with the national interest, was not indispensable because there was the alternative of diplomacy. It rarely happens that warfare is neither required for, nor detrimental to, national security—the only kind of situation in which the question whether to go to war would be a moral issue.

A recent book, entitled *On War and Morality*, focuses on "the question whether war in the modern world can be morally justified," and answers "by arguing that it cannot" (Holmes 1989, xi). True, war cannot be *morally* justified. This does not imply that "we do not have to wage war" (3) and that "the alternative is . . . to cease waging wars" (268). War, while not morally right, is sometimes an unfortunate *necessity*. Given our world is divided into independent states, "This state of affairs can be changed only by reconstituting societies," by making "peace education a priority," and by converting economies "to peaceful ends" (269). But surely, it is not within the power of governments or people, in authoritarian and even in democratic societies, to bring about such radical changes, even if there were the will to do so. Indulging in such utopian dreams is hardly helpful in solving our present predicaments.

2. Conduct of War

War, it seems, is the very opposite of law and morality. Yet there is an important tradition of legal and moral principles aiming at reducing the disasters of war once combat has started. Traditionally, these principles have been divided into rules of discrimination and rules of proportionality.

Perhaps the most important rule of discrimination is that of noncombatant immunity. While the killing of soldiers and the destruction of military targets is legitimate in a "just" war, it is prohibited to kill or to harm "innocent" civilians deliberately; here "innocent" is used in the technical sense of not participating in military activities. In the words of the pastoral letter of the U.S. National Conference of Catholic Bishops: "The lives of innocent persons may never be taken directly, regardless of the purpose alleged for doing so," as they are "caught up in a war not of their making" (U.S. Catholic Bishops 1985, 265). The U.S. Army *Field Manual* stipulates that "a commander may not put his prisoners to death because their presence retards his movements" (quoted by Brandt 1974, 27). Prohibitions to bomb hospitals or historic monuments fall under the same category. The rule of noncombatant immunity prohibits nuclear or biological or chemical warfare because these are weapons of indiscriminate mass destruction (Nagel 1974, 19). This is, clearly, a deontological principle; its prohibitions are absolute, allowing for no exceptions because of the consequences of its application.[5] However, some deontologists, especially those within the Christian tradition, make an exception by invoking the "doctrine of double effect" that concerns actions with both good and bad consequences (hence the name), such as using bad means to bring about a good end. According to this doctrine, it is morally legitimate to use the former, provided one foresees their undesirable consequences, but does not intend to bring them about. Accordingly, it is wrong to kill innocent civilians intentionally to win a just war, but permissible to do so knowingly, but without the specific intention to kill them. A bomber pilot is then morally entitled to bomb a factory, even if he realizes that his act will cause the death of many civilians nearby, provided his intention is to hasten victory; but he is not permitted to perform the very same action if he deliberately intends to victimize nearby civilians.[6]

While the principle of discrimination prohibits the intentional harming of noncombatants, the principle of proportionality is directed against inflicting harm quite generally, including the non-deliberate but foreseeable harm to civilians, but only to the extent that the damage done is out of proportion to the goal of bringing the war to a victorious end. To quote the Conference of Catholic Bishops again: "The damage to be inflicted and the costs incurred by war must be proportionate to the good expected by taking up arms" (U.S. Catholic Bishops 1985, 255). Thus, killing civilians as a nondeliberate but anticipated side effect in the course of an air strike on military installations is legitimate, provided doing so is a necessary means to the "good" of victory. In this vein, the U.S. Army *Field Manual* dealing with limitations of strategic bombing stipulates that "loss of life and damage to property must not be out of proportion to the military advantage to be gained" (quoted by Brandt 1974, 28). Unlike the principle of discrimination and of double effect, that of proportionality is one of consequential and, more particularly, of utilitarian ethics. To achieve the greatest possible balance of good over evil, it is legitimate to secure the greater good by means of the lesser evil, for example, to win the war by victimizing civilians during an air strike on military targets, provided the harm inflicted on the innocent does not outweigh the benefit of victory. Some writers combine the deontological with the consequential approach. Thus, Michael Walzer supplements his deontological position by a utilitarian escape clause "to work out those special cases where victory is so important or defeat so frightening that it is morally, as well as militarily, necessary to override the rules of war" (Walzer 1977, 132). Walzer character- izes his view as "the utilitarianism of extremity, for it concedes that in certain very special cases, though never as a matter of course even in just wars, the only restraints upon military action are those of usefulness and proportionality" (231).[7]

Here we are again faced with the difficulty of applying such rules to concrete situations. The distinctions between combatants and noncombatants have been blurred in modern warfare. Do the latter include workers in food processing plants or farmers? (See Walzer 1977, 146.) Is the shooting of hostages (and of how many?) in reprisal proportionate to the military necessity of deterring further partisan or guerilla activity? How can one estimate the probability of the number of civilians killed in an air raid on a munitions factory against the probability that the damage "will significantly enhance the prospect of victory"? (Brandt 1974, 36). Which of the two principles is applicable when they come into conflict? The rule of noncombatant immunity prohibits the torture of prisoners to extract information even of significant military importance; but the rule of proportionality might permit such repulsive measures as a necessary evil.[8]

Obviously, principles of permissible and prohibited conduct in war are meant to provide only general guidelines. Still, our funda- mental question remains: What is the range of their relevance?

A commanding officer cannot reasonably make strategic or tactical decisions in disregard of military outcomes. Therefore, I do not think that deontological considerations such as the principle of discrimination or of double effect are applicable to the conduct of war; but compliance with such deontological norms is often in a nation's interest.

The consequentialist principle of proportionality is clearly rele- vant to damage inflicted without military necessity. Such actions are wrong, because alternative, less harmful means to winning the war are clearly available without doing such harm. The rule of proportionality relevantly prohibits the committing of war crimes, such as wanton destruction,[9] indiscriminate terror bombing, deportation of slave labor, taking of hostages, plunder, and rape; and the greater the harm, the worse the crime. Such actions are often motivated by hate and revenge; but they are wrong, not because they are done intentionally, but because they are avoidable and, hence, strategically unnecessary. "To assign paramountcy to national interest commits one to the rationalization of *any* magnitude of evil that circumstances might render necessary to protect that interest" (Holmes 1989, 82); yes, but not of any evil *not* indispensable for that purpose.

Let us suppose now that a country is fighting for its very survival, and that it becomes necessary to bomb population centers to demoralize the enemy or to torture prisoners to extract important information. Such policies are condemned by the rules of discrimination and of double effect. But the principle of proportionality would sanction such actions, provided that they are really indispensable to achieving victory. Considerations of proportionality are, indeed, relevant here. They are applicable, however, as a principle, not of morality, but of rationality. Given the practically necessary goal of national survival, such measures may be rational—deplorable yes, but not immoral, and of course not moral either. This simply illustrates that "war is hell," and had better be avoided by all means.

There are, however, situations that are less clear-cut, and therefore more difficult to resolve, like the atomic bombing of Hiroshima or the fire bombing of Dresden. Defenders of these actions argue that they were the only effective way to bring the war to an early victorious end. Critics maintain that means to avoid these innumerable civilian casualties were available as a "second best" policy, and could invoke the moral principle (advanced in the preceding chapter) that one ought to pay a small price in effectiveness to avoid inflicting great harm.

At the other extreme, there is a war fought not for survival, but for imperialistic, territorial expansion. Such a war is itself wrong, and so are all warlike actions taken by the aggressor nation, even those that otherwise would be permitted by the principle of proportionality. Germany's bombing of Rotterdam and Birmingham was wrong, regardless of whether these actions contributed significantly to Germany's war effort. Somewhere between these extremes one could situate wars not necessary for survival, but not imperialistic either, like the United States's invasion of Panama, and wars the government mistakenly believes to be required by the national interest, like the United States's Vietnam venture. No doubt, the Me Lai massacre and the use of napalm were highly immoral. But what about measures that were militarily necessary, given America's war aims? One could argue that they were, not morally right, but rational with respect to the national interest, as it was conceived by the government, however mistakenly. One could also maintain that these military actions were morally wrong because they were not required by America's real interest. I must leave this question open.

Now, conforming to the moral principle of proportionality and even of noncombatant immunity is often in the interest of belligerents, and therefore an instance of morality being the best policy. I mentioned in that connection (chapter 4, When Moral Judgments Are Counterproductive) the Hague convention on prisoners of war. For example, Germany respected these rules during the Second World War, at least with respect to prisoners of war of Western nations, even if they were Jewish. Nazi Germany did not adopt this policy for moral reasons (in spite of its ideology), but out of self-interest, especially when, after the Africa campaign, German prisoners in large numbers fell into Allied hands.[10]

It is rational for nations to adopt conventions prohibiting the mistreatment of prisoners of war, the use of poison gas and biological weapons, and, of course, of nuclear arms, and to comply with them once war has broken out, provided they have good reason to believe that their opponents will also do so.

> Such absolute prohibitions might conceivably be defended in terms of long-range utility: all states, it might be argued, would be better off in the long run if they were to accept the short-run military disadvantages that acceptance of such restraints might produce in particular circumstances. (Nardin 1983, 294)

Richard Brandt justifies such deontological principles by a rule-utilitarian approach.[11] Long-range utilitarian considerations make it rational for nations to adopt such rules of war, and "immediate expediency is not a moral justification for infringing the rules" (Brandt 1974, 27). Yet Brandt, like Walzer, has an act-utilitarian escape clause, namely, "the restriction that the rules of war may not prevent a belligerent from using all the power necessary to overcome the enemy" (Brandt 1974, 32). According to the previous considerations, these are matters of rationality, not of utilitarian morality.

I have been concerned in this chapter exclusively with the relevance of ethics to military policy of *states* at war, not with choices facing *individuals* in a country involved in hostilities, for example, whether to answer the draft call or to take a stand as a conscientious objector, or whether, as a soldier, to "follow orders" considered wrong. These are, of course, genuine moral issues.

Notes

1. He expanded his theory subsequently in "The Moral Standing of States" (Walzer 1980).
2. I shall not deal explicitly with Walzer's two other conditions under which *A* may justly invade *B*: "to assist secessionist movements" in *B* and "to balance the prior intervention of other powers" in a civil war within *B* (Walzer 1977, 108).
3. "Indeed, the history, culture, and religion of a community may be such that authoritarian regimes come, as it were, naturally, reflecting a widely shared world view or way of life" (Walzer 1980, 225).
4. Jeff McMahan expresses the same view: "If a state lacked domestic legitimacy—that is, if it had no right to govern—what reason could there be to protect *it* (as distinct from the people) from external coercion?" (McMahan 1985, 34).
5. "If it is not allowable to *do* certain things, such as killing unarmed prisoners or civilians, then no argument about what will happen if one doesn't do them can show that doing them would be all right" (Nagel 1976, 8).
6. The doctrine of double effect is criticized by Holmes: "If one prohibits the killing of innocents, he cannot then invoke good intentions to justify proceeding to kill them" (200).
7. This approach has been criticized as a "hybrid morality that relies on authoritative rules for ordinary situations but allows instrumental or utilitarian calculation in certain extraordinary or extreme situations" (Nardin 1983, 296).
8. Nagel, a proponent of deontological morality in this area, recognizes the possibility of such a conflict (Nagel 1974, 23).

9. According to the U.S. *Army Field Manual*, "the measure of permissible devastation is found in the strict necessities of war. Devastation as an aim in itself or as a separate measure of war is not sanctioned by the law of war. There must be some reasonably close connection between the destruction of property and the overcoming of the enemy's army" (quoted by Brandt 1974, 38).

10. Mutual trust was lacking between Germany and Russia, and both nations treated each other's prisoners-of-war badly.

11. While act-utilitarianism enjoins us to choose the *action* most likely to promote the general good of everyone, rule-utilitarianism requires us to act according to the *rule* most likely to have utilitarian consequences (e.g., always to tell the truth), even if acting according to the rule fails to do so in particular circumstances (e.g., even when telling the truth has undesirable consequences) (cf. Frankena 1973, 39).

6
Morality and Nuclear Deterrence

The question whether nuclear deterrence is morally right or wrong has been discussed in numerous books and articles. As in the previous chapters, I shall not take sides, but focus on the problem of the relevance of such moral judgments. I shall therefore concentrate on the *moral* arguments in favor of and against nuclear deterrence, without getting involved in the highly technical aspects of nuclear strategy (which I would not be competent to discuss). Nor shall I dwell on the horrors of nuclear warfare, from fallout to the possible end of our civilization; they are being evoked daily, and convincingly.

Let us take two nuclear powers: to get away from the obsolete cold war perspective, let us call them A (the attacker) and D (the deterrer).[1] That D adopts a policy of nuclear deterrence refers to the following: D foresees the possibility that A might launch a nuclear attack (a first strike) against D. D therefore *intends* to launch a retaliatory nuclear strike against A (a second strike)— and explicitly or implicitly threatens that he will—*should A* make such an attack. D expects that his conditional intention will persuade A that the costs of a nuclear aggression would be higher than any possible benefits, and that A will therefore refrain from initiating a nuclear strike against D. In the words of Robert McNamara: "Nuclear weapons are totally useless—except only to deter one's opponent from using them" (McNamara 1983, 79).

Two moral questions are involved:

1. Is it morally right or wrong for D to form the intention to retaliate against A with nuclear weapons, should A launch a nuclear attack against D?

2. If *D*'s attempt at deterrence fails, and *A* strikes, is it morally right or wrong for *D* to carry out his conditional intention, that is, to retaliate against *A*?

1. Moral Arguments for and against Deterrence and Retaliation

Deontological Arguments

How do moralists of the deontologist persuasion answer the second question? If *D*'s efforts at deterring *A* from nuclear aggression fail, and *A* does attack *D* with nuclear weapons, is *D* morally entitled to avail himself of his remaining nuclear arsenal and to retaliate against *A*? Many deontologists answer negatively. "If deterrence is successful, the 'use' that is required never occurs. If deterrence is unsuccessful, the use that does occur is . . . murderous and profoundly wrong" (Wasserstrom 1985, 440). Using nuclear weapons is "absolutely reprehensible morally" (Ullman 1985, 570) and "impermissible whatever the consequences" (Morris 1985, 483).

Nuclear warfare in general is deemed wrong because it necessarily violates the traditional norms of *ius in bello,* especially the principle of noncombatant immunity. These prohibitions apply most clearly to countervalue strategies, the indiscriminate bombing of population centers. As proclaimed by the U.S. Catholic Bishops in 1982:

> Under no circumstances may nuclear weapons . . . be used for the purpose of destroying population centers or other predominantly civilian targets. . . . Retaliatory action . . . which would indiscriminately take many wholly innocent lives . . . must also be condemned. (U.S. Catholic Bishops 1985, 267)

But even counterforce strategies aimed specifically at military targets necessarily violate this just war principle, because any use of nuclear weapons is bound to cause innumerable civilian victims as well. Thus, the U.S. Catholic Bishops are "highly skeptical" (1985, 267) about the possibility of limiting nuclear strikes to military objectives. This is one reason for the radical difference, even on the moral level, between conventional and nuclear warfare.

Retaliation has been found to be incompatible with several deontological principles of Kantian ethics, such as the moral obligation to treat all innocent persons as ends and not merely as means, and to be willing to be on the receiving as well as on the giving end of our actions (Werner 1987, 160). Retaliation has also been condemned as violating the Socratic principle that it is better to suffer wrong than to do wrong (Kenny 1985, 66).

Some of the deontologists who condemn retaliation explicitly argue for the alternative: "Suppose that deterrence breaks down: . . . then obviously the only thing to do is to surrender" (Kenny 1985, 56).

Other moralists of the deontological persuasion take the opposite view, by invoking a different moral principle: *D*'s retaliatory strike is justified by virtue of the moral right of self-defense (Bobbitt 1987, 120), judged to have a greater moral weight than the duty not to victimize innocent civilians.

As to the first of the two moral problems: Is it justified to intend and possibly to threaten nuclear war to prevent nuclear war? No, according to many deontologists, because of the moral principle that it is wrong to intend, even conditionally, to do what it would be wrong to do (McMahan 1985, 523). Since deterrence involves the intention, however conditional, to victimize innumerable innocents, "nuclear deterrence is deemed immoral, even if it is successful and nuclear weapons are never used" (McMahan 1985, 577), and regardless of "whether national self-interest is enhanced or not" (Donaldson 1985, 548). Indeed, it has been argued that deterrence cannot be credible unless it involves threats against population centers, and hence the (conditional) intention to kill innocent civilians (Finnis, Boyle, & Grisez 1987, 138). Kantian ethics is invoked in this connection as well: "For the Kantian, to intend that which is forbidden is to be willing to act in a manner which is ruled out by the Cathegorical Imperative. The intent is wrong quite independently of its being linked to future effects" (Dworkin 1985, 447). Furthermore, forming the intention to use nuclear weapons, if only for retaliatory purposes, involves the risk that they might be used; but it is wrong to risk doing, as well as to intend to do, wrong (McMahan 1985, 535). What if *D* threatens *A* with retaliation but does not intend to retaliate in case *A* attacks? That, too, is considered wrong because it constitutes deception, which is wrong in principle (McMahan 1985, 520).

These are examples of the view that deterrence as well as actual retaliation are immoral. Other deontological moralists take the opposite position, that both are morally right. Thus, the right of self-defense has been invoked to justify deterrence as well as retaliation.

> If it is legitimate for nations to provide for their self-defense, then the United States is justified in devising a nuclear strategy because there are situations in which the U.S. self-defense cannot be maintained without a nuclear deterrent. (Bobbitt 1987, 120)[2]

Some writers take an intermediary position: retaliation is wrong, but deterrence is right. We have seen that the U.S. Catholic Bishops condemn the *use* of nuclear weapons, even for retaliatory purposes. Yet they come out for a "strictly conditional" moral acceptance of deterrence, provided this policy is adopted "only to prevent the use of nuclear weapons by others" (U.S. Catholic Bishops 1985, 272). Actual retaliation is immoral, but the conditional intention to retaliate is moral. Gregory Kavka explicitly espouses this "paradox of deterrence." He holds both that "it would be wrong to retaliate if the offense were committed" (Kavka 1987, 33) because it would involve the killing of innumerable innocents (80), *and* that "it is permissible to form the intention to retaliate should the offense be committed" (33) because of the right of national self-defense (81). Kavka rejects the deontological principle that it is always wrong to intend to do what would be wrong to do. He considers it permissible to form the conditional intention to perform the impermissible act of retaliation if that intention is "adopted solely to prevent the circumstances in which the intention would be acted upon" (82), namely, a nuclear attack by *A*. "Thus it seems, incredibly, that it may be right to form the conditional intention, wrong to fulfill it. That is the paradox" (Lewis 1984, 141). Whether this paradoxical view is also an inconsistent one, I shall examine later.

Consequential Arguments

Some moralists of the consequentialist school consider all nuclear warfare immoral because of the horrendous effects which, they feel, cannot be counterbalanced by any possible benefit. More specifically, retaliation violates the utilitarian standard that all individuals who are affected by an action are to count equally.

> I do not see how it could be thought right rather than wrong, better rather than worse, that, say, tens or hundreds of millions of the inhabitants of the Soviet Union . . . be deliberately killed by a nuclear attack so that those of us in the United States and elsewhere should not be either dead or red, if that is in fact the only choice at hand. (Wasserstrom 1985, 432)

Furthermore, if *D*'s deterrence fails and *A* attacks, it might be senseless for *D* to use his remaining nuclear weapons to launch a retaliatory counterattack against *A*, thereby increasing the probability of total nuclear war. "Any use of nuclear weapons . . . carries with it the high and inescapable risk of escalation into the general nuclear war which would bring ruin to all and victory to none" (Bundy et al., 757).

Other authors take the opposite view, that *D*'s retaliatory strike will *reduce* the likelihood of total nuclear war between *A* and *D*. This long-range benefit, they argue, outweighs the immediate calamities (for both *A* and *D*) resulting from *D*'s use of nuclear arms. "There are some circumstances in which a limited use of nuclear weapons would be morally justified," specifically if "a limited retaliatory strike was the best way of avoiding a significantly greater evil" (Sterba 1987, 125), such as a massive nuclear counterattack by *A*.

Consequentialists make different predictions with respect to the outcome of deterrence as well as of retaliation, and that is the reason why they disagree as to the morality of the former as well as of the latter. Some hold that *D*'s conditional intention to use nuclear weapons carries with it the danger that *D* will actually use them. "Making threats credible makes nuclear use more likely" (Van Gelder 1989, 177), that is, use by *D*. But "if threats are not credible, deterrence fails" (177) and it is *A* who might be tempted to strike. Indeed, *A* is likely to discover that *D* is likely to realize that retaliation is likely to lead to nuclear escalation: therefore, *A* is unlikely to take *D*'s conditional intention seriously; therefore, *D*'s strategy lacks credibility; therefore, *A* can safely attack. "Nuclear deterrence appears to be either incredible or self-defeating; either way, it fails to prevent nuclear conflict" (159).

Ethical thinkers who consider deterrence immoral for consequentialist reasons are more likely to argue that we cannot figure out probabilities of outcomes in nuclear matters and that, under conditions of uncertainty, one had best choose the lesser evil, that is, apply the maximin rule. Now, the worst possible consequence of adopting a nuclear deterrence strategy is the outbreak of nuclear war with *its* worst consequences. On the other hand, if D gives up its nuclear arsenal but A remains a nuclear power, A has no reason to launch a nuclear attack against D. The worst that could happen is A's domination of D, leading perhaps to D's loss of its national independence—a lesser evil (and very much so) compared with a nuclear holocaust. Abandoning nuclear weapons, even unilaterally, thus saves innumerable lives, and is "therefore morally mandatory" (Goodin 1985, 655) as well as rational.

Other moralists of the consequentialist persuasion hold that probabilities in this area can at least be estimated and must be taken into account. They believe that deterrence is likely to be successful and to constitute, therefore, the best possible protection against nuclear war. They point to the long period of nuclear peace since World War II as a result of the balance of mutual deterrence between the nuclear powers. Gregory Kavka, for example, while not excluding the possibility of nuclear war if D adopts a deterrence strategy, estimates its probability much lower than the likelihood that D loses his national independence as a consequence of his policy of doing away with nuclear weapons. Hence, in comparing the two policies, "the utilitarian seems trapped between the Scylla of a smaller risk of a worse disaster (that is, full-scale nuclear war) and the Charybdis of a greater risk of a smaller disaster (that is, a nuclear strike or Soviet domination via blackmail)" (Kavka 1983, 255). Kavka concludes that "minimum deterrence is more rational than unilateral disarmament and hence is morally permissible" (Kavka 1987, 70), thus overriding his own deontological objection against deterrence that it threatens innocent civilians. In the words of Michael Walzer: "We threaten evil in order not to do it, and the doing of it would be so terrible that the threat seems in comparison to be morally defensible" (Walzer 1977, 274).

2. Are Such Moral Arguments Relevant?

My answer to the question of the relevance of moral considerations to nuclear deterrence will be based on the conclusions of the previous chapters. To recapitulate: Moral injunctions apply to agents in situations of choice. There is no point in giving moral advice to an agent to act in a certain way if to do so is practically impossible or practically necessary. In a system of independent states, statesmen have practically no choice but to aim at the protection of their states' military security and national independence; to do so is rational, but neither right nor wrong. In a system of independent nuclear powers, it is rational for each to adopt the optimal nuclear strategy with respect to its national defense and national survival, but not rational to embark, for moral reasons, on policies less adequate or detrimental to military security and national interest.

It follows that it is pointless for academic writers to urge political leaders to comply in nuclear matters with general moral principles prohibiting or favoring nuclear deterrence. Deontological principles, inapplicable to the conduct of war in general (see chapter 5, Conduct of War), are surely irrelevant to nuclear policies. If deterrence or retaliation (in case deterrence fails) is the optimal strategy in a given situation, it would not be rational to decide against it in order to comply with some deontological norm, "regardless of consequences," and "whether national self-interest is enhanced or not," and, more specifically, to conform to the principle that it is wrong to intend to do wrong, or worse to do wrong than to suffer wrong. It is just as pointless to *justify* deterrence by such deontological principles as the moral right of self-defense, rather than by its usefulness. Nor is it relevant to ask: Is D morally permitted to intend to retaliate should A attack, but morally prohibited from retaliating if A actually attacks? The pertinent question is: Is it *rational* to intend to retaliate and not actually to do so? The answer may well be affirmative; it "may serve one's ends to form an intention that it would not serve one's ends to fulfill" (Lewis 1984, 141). Paradoxical as it may seem, there is no inconsistency.[3]

The decision whether to adopt a policy of deterrence and of retaliation surely depends on the probable consequences. This does not imply, however, that norms of consequential *ethics* are any more relevant than principles of deontological morality. If "minimum deterrence is more rational than unilateral disarmament," it does not follow that it is "hence, morally permissible." If deterrence is the best policy from the point of view of military security, there is no point in claiming either that this policy is moral, or that it is immoral because, for example, it violates the utilitarian principle that all persons should be treated equally (in *A* as well as in *D*). If, on the contrary, deterrence, especially if it is mutual, increases the probability of nuclear war and mutual annihilation, this strategy is militarily unacceptable, and moral considerations are, again, beside the point. If the prediction is warranted that unilateral nuclear disarmament eliminates the danger of nuclear war while somehow preserving *D*'s national independence, it follows, not that it is "therefore morally mandatory," but that it is the rational thing to do. However, *D*'s abandonment of its nuclear arsenal is more likely to lead, ultimately if not immediately, to *A*'s domination over *D* without a nuclear fight. But to surrender—"the only thing to do"—is the only thing a government cannot reasonably do as long as maintaining its national independence remains a possibility, and therefore a practical necessity.

We have seen, in chapter 4, that ethical considerations are relevant when government officials are faced with the choice of policies equally conducive to the national interest. Accordingly, if alternative nuclear policies are available to *D* providing comparative levels of military security, it is relevant to recommend the morally preferable deterrence strategy. If U.S. national security could have been protected just as well without deployment of MIRVed missiles, it is appropriate to criticize the government for having adopted immoral measures—immoral because not indispensable for defense and deterrence; and such criticism might influence it to reduce its nuclear armaments to its necessary minimum in the future. The same moral criticism could be leveled against the Star Wars program which, although perhaps compatible with military security, does not improve it, as many argue. (Others consider it detrimental, and likely to trigger off an SDI armaments race.) Curiously, most writers who judge nuclear deterrence by ethical criteria fail to deal with the possibility of alternative strategies, the only situation to which moral considerations seem to me relevant, and fail to apply the *ethical* standard that it is wrong to have a stronger (and more expensive) defense system than required for national security. For example, it seems to me that even the title of one of the many recent collections of essays on ethics and nuclear policies, *Nuclear Rights/Nuclear Wrongs*, points in the wrong direction. According to the introduction, these writings deal with the question, "Which uses or threats to use nuclear weapons . . . are justified on the basis of moral, philosophical reasoning" and which policies are "prohibited by considerations of moral philosophy"? (Paul et al. 1986, vii). Yet, most of these essays do not deal with the question *which* of several available uses or threats are morally justified. When there is no choice, moral-philosophical reasoning is not relevant, except to show that normative ethics is irrelevant, because nuclear policies are neither right nor wrong, but either rational or not rational.

3. Discussion of Possible Objections

The difficulties of predicting outcomes of contemplated foreign policies are magnified when it comes to deciding whether to adopt a strategy of nuclear deterrence. Will *D*'s policy of deterrence preserve peace, or will it encourage *D* to avail himself of his nuclear arsenal, or does it lack credibility and will therefore encourage *A* to launch a nuclear attack? How high or low is the probability of nuclear war as a consequence of *D*'s deterrence in comparison with the likelihood that *A* will dominate *D* as a result of *D*'s nuclear disarmament? Does the retaliatory strategy of counterforce lessen or increase the probability of nuclear exchange compared with the older countervalue strategy?[4] I would not minimize the tremendous difficulties of making such predictions. The topic does not require me to participate in these controversies, as these are issues of military strategy, not of ethics.

It may be objected that I have dealt with nuclear deterrence as if unilateral nuclear disarmament with the danger to national survival were the only alternative. Yet, there is the further, and most desirable, possibility that *A* and *D* conclude treaties, if not of nuclear disarmament, at least of nuclear weapons reduction. However, such agreements would be the result of joint decisions of nuclear powers, and game theory considerations are applicable. If mutual trust between *A* and *D* is lacking, there is no use advising *D*'s government (or *A*'s) to conclude such a treaty on moral grounds. If there are good reasons for cooperating, it is rational for *D* (and *A*) to enter into negotiations—another example of morality being good policy.

Similarly, in most situations it will be in *D*'s national interest to avoid the use of nuclear arms and, if retaliation becomes necessary, to limit its destructive effects as much as possible, in order to lessen the danger that *A* might counterretaliate out of revenge. "If the United States ever uses nuclear weapons it should (morally) aim these weapons at Soviet military targets and not at the Soviet population" (Foelber 1989, 124). Yes, but let us strike out "morally," even in parentheses.

There is a further possible objection: True, nuclear deterrence policies have been judged right or wrong by different moral standards. But there is no less disagreement among military strategists as to which nuclear policy is the soundest. The reason for rejecting moral criteria in this area is not their diversity, but the irrelevance of ethical judgments to courses of action judged—rightly or wrongly—to be the most effective means to a practically necessary goal.

To adopt the most effective foreign, including nuclear, policy is rational for *government*, but not for ethnic or religious minorities or for ideological or political movements alienated from the political system under which they live. Such groups may give priority to saving lives at any price or even welcome foreign domination. Even citizens with a stake in their nation's continued independence may reasonably have other priorities. Thus, soldiers, ordered to drop a nuclear device, are faced with a genuine *moral* dilemma whether to "follow orders." Citizens may be morally responsible for their own choices; but are they accountable for their government's nuclear policies? It has been claimed that "in an era when weapons of mass destruction enable nation-states to wreck havoc upon whole continents, citizens simply must be held responsible for how their nations behave in regard to the use of these weapons" (Child 1987, 70), and that citizens, even in a dictatorship, who "allow" their government to launch a nuclear attack "lose their right not to be put at risk" by the opposing power (71). Yet, a decision to "pull the nuclear trigger" would have to be made on the spur of a moment at the top without the possibility to consult even legislators, let alone citizens. Even in democracies, general nuclear policies are formed by the executive or the chiefs of staff, and citizens have no say, and hence, no moral responsibility.

As mentioned at several places in this study, I am far from claiming that governments do in fact always act rationally in the area of foreign policy. This applies also to nuclear strategy. Under the influence of interest groups (e.g., the military establishment) public officials often make decisions that are perhaps rational in view of their goal of staying in power at home, but not rational with respect to their necessary goal of achieving security at the international level. But it is hard to imagine that foreign policy decision makers will actually be influenced in their nuclear policies by moral considerations such as Kantian or utilitarian norms or the right (rather than the necessity) of self-defense or the wrongness of intending to do wrong or even the prohibition to victimize noncombatants. Writers can give useful advice to governmental leaders as to the *rationality* of nuclear policies; their moral pronouncements are likely to fall on deaf ears.

I have tried to show that social scientists and philosophers condemning certain nuclear policies as immoral may well dissuade government from acting rationally, and that writers morally approving of these policies influence government in favor of strategies which they have sufficient rational reasons to adopt. "Satisfaction of both military criteria and moral criteria is necessary for an acceptable deterrence policy" (Shue 1986, 48), but only in the rare case when several deterrence policies are equally acceptable by military criteria.

Notes

1. I am following the example of Van Gelder, 1989.
2. This passage does not specify whether this moral permission applies also to the Soviet Union, or generally to every nuclear power.
3. This is denied, for example, by Gauthier (1984, 101–22).
4. "It is argued both that smaller, less-destructive limited options make nuclear war less 'unthinkable' and therefore more likely . . . and that they make a threat to retaliate more credible and thus enhance deterrence and make war less likely" (Powell 1989, 504).

Some Sobering Conclusions

We are trapped in an anarchical system of about 150 states with often arbitrary borders, the result of historical accidents. This system is not static. Older nations are merging into larger combinations or breaking up into smaller units asserting their own independence. Newer states sometimes want to modify their relations with other powers to the advantage of their own nation or tribe or ruling group.

It has been held that "within the modern state system it is a settled norm that the *preservation of the society of states itself is a good*" (Frost 1986, 121), and that "*patriotism* is a good thing" (Frost 1986, 124). This is by no means a settled matter. Some consider our present anarchical society of states an unfortunate reality. It is seen as a fertile ground for patriotism, a *bad* thing fostering the feeling of national superiority, national rivalries, and international conflict. Some even feel that the present system of states ought not to be preserved. Robert Hutchins argued that "because world government is necessary, it is therefore possible" (quoted by Thompson 1990, 164)—a glaring example of wishful thinking. World government is possible if one nation achieves world domination; but that would be considered by "world federalists" worse than the present precarious balance of power between independent states. To alter it is not within the capacity of statesmen or other individuals or groups at the present time.

The argument here has been that, given the present state system, governments have practically no choice but to aim at the promotion of the national interest, and often little choice but to enact the single most effective policy in view of that necessary goal. Since moral prescriptions are relevant only when there are genuine choices, a wide range of international politics falls outside the purview of ethics.

Even so, writers often proclaim that "morality should control relations among states" (Meyers 1987, 11). Is this an injunction meant to guide the conduct of statesmen? Should they be guided by morality even if it conflicts with the national interest? Guided by morality *tout court*? There are conflicting moral points of view even within our own culture: that the national interest itself is moral (even though its pursuit is practically unavoidable) *or* that different goals should take precedence; that states ought not to interfere in the domestic affairs of other states *or* that democratic states should spread these values among other nations by overt or even covert means; that military forces should be used only in self-defense *or* also to defend other states when their security or free institutions are endangered; that nuclear deterrence is morally justi-fied *or* that it is wrong.

Moral standards differ not only among ourselves; ethical norms different from ours are prevalent elsewhere. Fascism or National Socialism, abhorrent to us, have invoked their own moral principles (often disguised under the mask of "true" democracy). The impor-tance of these doctrines has diminished, and so has communism as a moral ideal. But today various religious fundamentalisms are on the increase, often coupled with expansionist nationalism with *its* morality. It is by no means "*settled* that any attempt by one state to achieve preponderance of power over other states is a bad thing"; nor is it true that "peace is regarded as a *settled* norm" (Frost 1986, 123; italics added). Attempts at establishing preponderance, even by war, easily finds its moral justification.

"Moral values and standards can make the world better" (M. Singer 1979, 143). Whose moral values? Surely not "theirs." But not "our" moral standards either. As we have seen, being guided by moral principles in foreign policy easily leads to an attitude of self-righteousness that may endanger the national interest and—at least indirectly—the safeguarding of these very moral principles.

> Laying down the moral law to sinning brethren from our seat of judgment no doubt pleases our own sense of rectitude. But it fosters dangerous misconceptions about the nature of foreign policy. . . . Little has been more pernicious in international politics than excessive righteousness. (Schlesinger 1986, 73, 74)

We have seen, however, that governments often invoke morality as a smokescreen for policies judged to be in the national interest. Using ideology as a weapon in the international contest is sometimes effective, but involves the danger that people, and governments as well, mistake professed moral principles for actual goals. The end of the cold war and the relative decrease of the power of the "Big Two" has blunted these ideological weapons on both sides. Yet, in a collection of essays on *U.S. Defense Policy in an Era of Constrained Resources*, published in 1990, one can read that "the Iron Curtain still exists" (Burns 1990, 5), and that "the Soviet Union's probable goal is that of the renewal and 'moral purification' of socialism and a communist renaissance couched in terms of *perestroika* and *glasnost*" (Pfalzgraff, Jr. 1990, xiii). The Soviet Union "continues to pursue goals antithetical to our own" (Burns 1990, 5). Yes, but they *continue* to be *national interest* goals. These have been antithetical to the national interest of the United States in the past, and will no doubt sometimes be so in the future. However, there is now a trend toward more common interests between the two, and more conflicts between the national interest of the United States and other powers. Events like the Hitler-Stalin pact, American and British alliance with the Soviet Union in World War II, the shifting alliances among Arab nations today (to take only more recent examples) indicate that conflicts and cooperation among states had best be explained in terms of national interest, not by reference to moral principles invoked as ideological tools.

Because of the widespread inclination to view international politics as a Manichaean contest between good and evil, my emphasis has been on circumscribing the areas of foreign politics falling outside the range of moral relevance. However, morality does have its place. It is to the point to recommend the adoption of foreign policy goals *compatible* with the national interest on moral grounds, for example, to urge our government to induce other states to protect their citizens' basic rights, to contribute to the development of less-advanced countries, to cooperate with other states in improving the environment or in combating international terrorism and drug traffic. It is often in the nation's own interest to adopt such goals, and arguments of rationality render moral justification even here redundant. On the other hand, imperialism, sometimes compatible with national interest but (by definition) not required by it, is condemnable on moral grounds. Moral considerations are also relevant when there is a choice between several policies conducive to the national interest, even if that choice includes a policy judged "second best" but morally superior. It is to the point to condemn the infliction of damage without military necessity or to commit war crimes.

In the last analysis, we should not squander our moral energies where they can do no good (and may do some harm), but concentrate on areas of foreign policy where our moral commitments do matter, and their expression can make a difference.

References

Alger, Chadwick F. 1981. Foreign policies of U.S. politics. In *Perspectives on world politics*, ed. Michael Smith et al., 173–85. London: Croom Helm.

Ambrose, Stephen E. 1988. *Rise to globalism: American foreign policy since 1938.* 5th rev. ed. New York: Viking Penguin Books.

Arrow, Kenneth T. 1982. Current developments in the theory of social choice. In *Rational man and irrational society?*, ed. Brian Barry and Russell Hardin, 252–63. Beverly Hills, Calif.: Sage Publications.

Ashley, Richard K. 1986. The poverty of neorealism. In *Neorealism and its critics*, ed. Robert O. Keohane, 255–300. New York: Columbia University Press.

Baier, Kurt. 1958. *The moral point of view: A rational basis of ethics.* Ithaca, N.Y.: Cornell University Press.

Barry, Brian. 1986. Can states be moral? International morality and the compliance problem. In *Ethics and international relations*, ed. Anthony Ellis, 61–84. Manchester, England: Manchester University Press.

————. 1989. *Theories of justice.* Berkeley and Los Angeles: University of California Press.

Barry, Brian, and Russell Hardin. 1982. Epilogue. In *Rational man and irrational society?* ed. Brian Barry and Russell Hardin, 367–86. Beverly Hills, Calif.: Sage Publications.

Barry, Brian, and Douglas W. Rae. 1975. Political evaluation. In *Handbook of political science*, ed. Fred I. Greenstein and Nelson W. Polsby, 1: 337–401. Reading, Mass.: Addison-Wesley.

Bedau, Hugo A. 1979. Human rights and foreign assistance program. In *Human rights and U.S. foreign policy*, ed. Peter G. Brown and Douglas MacLean, 29–44. Lexington, Mass.: D. C. Heath.

Beitz, Charles R. 1979. *Political theory and international relations.* Princeton, N. J.: Princeton University Press.

Benn, Stanley I. 1967. State. In *The encyclopedia of philosophy*, 8: 6–11. New York: Macmillan Co./Free Press.

Bobbitt, Philip Chase. 1987. The ethic of nuclear deterrence. In *Political realism and international morality*, ed. Kenneth Kipnis and Diana Meyers, 109–21. Boulder, Colo.: Westview Press.

Brandt, Richard B. 1974. Utilitarianism and the rules of war. In *War and moral responsibility*, ed. Marshall Cohen et al., 25–45. Princeton, N.J.: Princeton University Press.

———. 1977. The concept of rationality in ethical and political theory. In *Nomos 17 Yearbook of the American Society for Political and Legal Philosophy* (Human Nature in Politics).

———. 1979. *A theory of the good and the right*. Oxford: Clarendon Press.

———. 1990. The science of man and wide reflective equilibrium. *Ethics* 100:259–78.

Braybrooke, David. 1968. *Three tests for democracy*. New York: Random House.

Braybrooke, David, and Charles E. Lindblom. 1963. *A strategy of decision*. New York: Free Press.

Brown, Peter G. 1979. ". . . in the national interest." In *Human rights and U.S. foreign policy*, ed. Peter G. Brown and Douglas MacLean, 161–71. Lexington, Mass.: Lexington Books.

Bundy, McGeorge. 1984. Existential deterrence and its consequences. In *The security gamble*, ed. Douglas MacLean, 3–13. Totowa, N. J.: Rowman & Allenheld.

———. 1988. *Danger and survival*. New York: Random House.

Bundy, McGeorge, George F. Kennan, Robert S. McNamara, and Gerard Smith. 1982. Nuclear weapons and the Atlantic alliance. *Foreign Affairs* 60: (Summer 1982): 754–68.

Burns, William F. 1990. The United States in a changing world. In *U.S. defense policy in an era of constrained resources*, ed. Robert J. Pfaltzgraff, Jr., and Richard H. Shultz, Jr., 1–12. Lexington, Mass.: Lexington Books.

Chamberlin, John R. 1989. Ethics and game theory. *Ethics and International Affairs* 3: 261–76.

Child, James W. 1987. Political responsibility and noncombatant liability. In *Political realism and international morality*, ed. Kenneth Kipnis and Diana Meyers, 61–74. Boulder, Colo.: Westview Press.

Cohen, Avner. 1987. Reflections on realism in the nuclear age. In *Political realism and international morality*, ed. Kenneth Kipnis and Diana Meyers, 220–38. Boulder, Colo.: Westview Press.

Cohen, Marshall. 1984. Moral scepticism and international relations. *Philosophy and Public Affairs* 13:299–346.

Coleman, Jules, and John Ferejohn. 1986. Democracy and social choice. *Ethics* 97:6–25.

Darwall, Stephen L. 1983. *Impartial reason*. Ithaca, N. Y.: Cornell University Press.

Destler, I. M. 1981. Organization and bureaucratic politics. In *Perspectives on world politics*, ed. Michael Smith et al., 158–72. London: Croom Helm.

Donaldson, Thomas. 1985. Nuclear deterrence and self-defense. *Ethics* 95:537–48.

Doppelt, Gerald. 1978. Walzer's theory of morality in international relations. *Philosophy and Public Affairs* 8:3–26.

Doyle, Michael W. 1987. Liberal institutions and international ethics. In *Political realism and international morality*, ed. Kenneth Kipnis and Diana Meyers, 185–211. Boulder, Colo.: Westview Press.

Dworkin, Gerald, 1985. Nuclear intentions. *Ethics* 95:445–60.

Elster, Jon. 1986. Introduction. In *Rational choice*, ed. Jon Elster, 1–33. New York: New York University Press.

———. 1989. *Solomonic judgments: Studies in the limitations of rationality*. Cambridge: Cambridge University Press.

Fairbanks, Jr., Charles H. 1982. The British campaign against the slave trade: An example of successful human rights policy. In *Human rights and American foreign policy*, ed. Fred E. Baumann, 87–135. Gambier, Ohio: Public Affairs Center of Kenyon College.

Finnis, John, Joseph M. Boyle, Jr., and Germain Grisez. 1987. *Nuclear deterrence, morality, and realism*. New York: Oxford University Press.

Foelber, Robert E. 1989. Deterrence and the moral uses of weapons. In *Nuclear deterrence and moral restraint*, ed. Henry Shue, 115–62. Cambridge: Cambridge University Press.

Frankena, William K. 1973. *Ethics*. 2d ed. Englewood Cliffs, N.J.: Prentice-Hall.

Frost, Mervyn. 1986. *Towards a normative theory of international relations*. Cambridge: Cambridge University Press.

Garnett, John C. 1984. *Common sense and the theory of international politics*. Albany: State University of New York Press.

Gauthier, David. 1984. Deterrence, maximization, and rationality. In *The security gamble: Deterrence in the nuclear age*, ed. Douglas MacLean, 101–22. Totowa, N.J.: Rowman & Allenheld.

George, Alexander L. 1980. *Presidential decision-making in foreign policy*. Boulder, Colo.: Westview Press.

Gilpin, Robert G. 1981. Three models of the future. In *Perspectives on world politics*, ed. Michael Smith et al., 398–412. London: Croom Held.

———. 1986. The richness of the tradition of political realism. In *Neorealism and its critics*, ed. Robert O. Keohane, 301–21. New York: Columbia University Press.

Goldman, Alvin I. 1970. *A theory of human action*. Englewood Cliffs, N.J.: Prentice-Hall.

Goodin, Robert E. 1982. *Political theory and public policy*. Chicago: University of Chicago Press.

———. 1985. Disarmament as a moral certainty. *Ethics* 95:641–58.

Hanrieder, Wolfram F. 1981. Dissolving international politics: Reflections on the nation-state. In *Perspectives on world politics*, ed. Michael Smith et al., 132–45. London: Croom Helm.

Hardin, Russell. 1985. Individual sanctions, collective benefits. In *Paradoxes of rationality and cooperation*, ed. Richmond Campbell and Lanning Sowden, 339–54. Vancouver, Canada: University of British Columbia Press.

Hare, R.M. 1963. *Freedom and reason*. London: Oxford University Press.

Hare, T.E., and C.B. Joynt. 1982. *Ethics and international affairs*. New York: St. Martin's Press.

Harman, Gilbert. 1977. *The nature of morality*. New York: Oxford University Press.

Harsanyi, John C. 1985. Does reason tell us what moral code to follow and, indeed, to follow any moral code at all? *Ethics* 96:42–55.

Hesse, Mary. 1967. Models and analogy in science. *Encyclopedia of philosophy 5*. New York: The Macmillan Co.: 354–59.

Hoffmann, Stanley. 1981. *Duties beyond borders*. Syracuse, N.Y.: Syracuse University Press.

Holmes, Robert L. 1989. *On war and morality*. Princeton, N.J.: Princeton University Press.

James, Susan. 1984. *The content of social explanation*. New York: Cambridge University Press.

Kavka, Gregory S. 1983. Doubts about unilateral disarmament. *Philosophy and Public Affairs* 12:255–60.

———. 1987. *Moral paradoxes of nuclear deterrence*. Cambridge: Cambridge University Press.

Kennan, George F. 1985. Morality and foreign policy. *Foreign Affairs* 64:205–18.

Kenny, Anthony. 1985. *The logic of deterrence*. Chicago: University of Chicago Press.

Keohane, Robert A. 1984. *After hegemony*. Princeton, N.J.: Princeton University Press.

Keohane, Robert O. 1986. Theory of world politics: Structural realism and beyond. In *Neorealism and its critics,* ed. Robert O. Keohane, 158–203. New York: Columbia University Press.

———. 1989. Closing the fairness-practice gap. *Ethics and International Affairs* 3:101–16.

Keohane, Robert O., and Joseph S. Nye. 1977. Power and inter-dependence. Boston: Little, Brown and Co.

Kipnis, Kenneth. 1987. Introduction to part two. In *Political realism and international morality*, ed. Kenneth Kipnis and Diana Meyers, 105–8. Boulder, Colo.: Westview Press.

Knorr, Klaus. 1975. *The power of nations: The political economy of international relations*. New York: Basic Books.

Lackey, Douglas P. 1984. *Moral principles and nuclear weapons*. Totowa, N.J.: Rowman & Allenheld.

Lewis, David. 1984. Devil's bargains and the real world. In *The security gamble*, ed. Douglas MacLean, 141–54. Totowa, N.J.: Rowman & Allenheld.

Luban, David. 1980. Just war and human rights. *Philosophy and Public Affairs* 9:160–81.

Lukes, Steven. 1986. The morality of sanctions. *Philosophy Forum* 18:177–84.

Luper-Foy, Steven, ed. 1988. *Problems of international justice*. Boulder, Colo.: Westview Press.

Mackie, J.L. 1977. *Ethics: Inventing right and wrong*. Harmondsworth, England: Penguin Books Ltd.

MacLean, Douglas. 1979. Constraints, goals, and moralism in foreign policy. In *Human rights and U.S. foreign policy*, ed. Peter G. Brown and Douglas MacLean, 93–108. Lexington, Mass.: D.C. Heath.

McMahan, Jeff. 1985. Deterrence and deontology. *Ethics* 95:517–36.

———. 1986. The ethics of international intervention. In *Ethics and international relations*, ed. Anthony Ellis, 24–51. Manchester, England: Manchester University Press.

McNamara, Robert S. 1983. The military role of nuclear weapons. *Foreign Affairs* 62:59–80.

Macpherson, C.B. 1973. *Democratic theory: Essays in retrieval*. Oxford: Clarendon Press.

Meyers, Diana T. 1987. Introduction to part one. In *Political realism and international morality*, ed. Kenneth Kipnis and Diana Meyers, 11–14. Boulder, Colo.: Westview Press.

Morgenthau, Hans J. 1952. Another "Great Debate": The national interest of the U.S. *American Political Science Review* 46:971–78.

———. 1973. *Politics among nations*. 5th ed. New York: Alfred A. Knopf.

Morris, Christopher W. 1985. A contractarian defense of nuclear deterrence. *Ethics* 95:479–96.

Morse, Edward L. 1981. The transformation in foreign policies. In *Perspectives on world politics*, ed. Michael Smith et al., 146–57. London: Croom Helm.

Nagel, Thomas. 1974. War and massacre. In *War and moral responsibility*, ed. Marshall Cohen et al., 3–24. Princeton, N.J.: Princeton University Press.

Nardin, Terry. 1983. *Law, morality, and the relations of states*. Princeton, N.J.: Princeton University Press.

Olson, Mancur. 1965. *The logic of collective action*. Cambridge: Harvard University Press.

Oppenheim, Felix E. 1968. *Moral principles in political philosophy*. New York: Random House.

———. 1981. *Political concepts: A reconstruction*. Chicago: University of Chicago Press; and Oxford: Basil Blackwell.

Oye, Kenneth A., ed. 1986. *Cooperation under anarchy*. Princeton, N.J.: Princeton University Press.

Parfit, Derek. 1986. *Reasons and persons*. Oxford: Oxford University Press.

Paul, Ellen Frankel, et al., eds. 1986. *Nuclear rights/nuclear wrongs*. Oxford: Basil Blackwell.

Pfaltzgraff, Robert L., Jr., and Richard H. Shultz, Jr. 1990 Introduction. In *U.S. defense policy in an era of constrained resources*, ed. Robert L. Pfaltzgraff, Jr., and Richard H. Shultz, Jr., xi–xix. Lexington, Mass.: Lexington Books.

Postbrief, Sam. 1981. Review of *The ethics of war*, by Barrie Paskins and Michael Dockrill. *Ethics* 91:863–65.

Powell, Robert. 1989. Nuclear deterrence and the strategy of limited retaliation. *American Political Science Review* 83:503–18.

Putnam, Hilary. 1981. *Reason, truth, and history*. Cambridge: Cambridge University Press.

Rapoport, Anatol. 1982. Prisoner's dilemma: Recollections and observations. In *Rational man and irrational society?*, ed. Brian Barry and Russell Hardin, 72–83. Beverly Hills, Calif.: Sage Publications.

Rawls, John. 1971. *A theory of justice*. Cambridge: Harvard University Press, Belknap Press.

Raz, Joseph, ed. 1978. *Practical reasoning*. Oxford: Oxford University Press.

Rosenau, James N. 1968. National interest. In *International Encyclopedia of the Social Sciences*, 5:34–40. New York: Macmillan Co./Free Press.

———. 1989. Global changes and theoretical challenges: Toward a postinternational politics for the 1990s. In *Global changes and theoretical challenges: Approaches to world politics for the 1990s*, ed. Ernst-Otto Czempiel and James N. Rosenau, 1–20. Lexington, Mass.: Lexington Books.

Rothstein, Robert L. 1981. On the costs of realism. In *Perspectives on world politics*, ed. Michael Smith et al., 388–97. London: Croom Helm.

Schlesinger, Arthur M., Jr. 1971. The necessity of amorality in foreign affairs. *Harper's Magazine*, August, 72–77.

———. 1986. *The cycles of American history*. Boston: Houghton Mifflin Company.

Schumpeter, Joseph A. 1951. *Imperialism and social classes*, trans. Heinz Norden. New York: A.M. Kelley.

Sen, Amartya K. 1977. Rational fools: A critique of the behavioral foundations of economic theory. *Philosophy and Public Affairs* 6:317–44.

———. 1982. *Choice, welfare, and measurement*. Cambridge: MIT Press.

———. 1987. *On ethics and economics*. Oxford: Basil Blackwell.

Shue, Henry. 1986. Two concepts of deterrence. In *Nuclear rights/ nuclear wrongs*, ed. Ellen Frankel Paul et al., 44–73. Oxford: Basil Blackwell.

Sick, Gary. 1989. Moral choice in the Iran-Iraq conflict. *Ethics and International Affairs* 3:117–34.

Simon, Herbert A. 1985. Human nature in politics: The dialogue of psychology with political science. *American Political Science Review* 79:293–304.

Singer, Max. 1990. Moral standards under pressure. *Ethics and International Affairs* 4:135–44.

Singer, Peter. 1979. Famine, affluence, and morality. In *Philosophy, politics, and society*, 5th series, ed. Peter Laslett and James Fishkin, 21–35. New Haven: Yale University Press.

Sinnott-Armstrong, Walter. 1984. "Ought" conversationally implies "can." *Philosophical Review* 93:249–61.

Smith, Michael T. 1989. Ethics and intervention. *Ethics and International Affairs* 3:1–26.

Sondermann, Fred A. 1983. The concept of the national interest. In *The theory and practice of international relations*, ed. William C. Olson et al., 57–65. Englewood Cliffs, N.J.: Prentice-Hall.

Sterba, James P. 1987. Between MAD and counterforce. In *Political realism and international morality*, ed. Kenneth Kipnis and Diana Meyers, 122–36. Boulder, Colo.: Westview Press.

Taylor, Michael. 1987. *The possibility of cooperation*. Cambridge: Cambridge University Press.

Thompson, Kenneth W. 1990. Peace studies: Social movement or intellectual discipline? *Ethics and International Affairs* 4:163–74.

Ullman, Richard. 1985. Denuclearizing international politics. *Ethics* 95:479–96.

U.S. Catholic Bishops. 1985. Pastoral letter on war and peace. In *Nuclear strategy, arms control, and the future*, ed. P. Edward Haley, David M. Keithly, and Jack Merritt, 263–75. Boulder, Colo.: Westview Press.

Van Gelder, Timothy T. 1989. Credible threats and usable weapons: Some dilemmas of deterrence. *Philosophy and Public Affairs* 18:158–83.

Waltz, Kenneth N. 1954. *Man, the state, and war.* New York: Columbia University Press.

———. 1979. *Theory of international politics.* New York: Random House.

Walzer, Michael. 1974. World War II: Why was this war different? In *War and moral responsibility*, ed. Marshall Cohen et al., 85–103. Princeton, N.J.: Princeton University Press.

———. 1977. *Just and unjust wars.* New York: Basic Books.

———. 1980. The moral standing of states: A response to four critics. *Philosophy and Public Affairs* 9:209–29.

Wasserstrom, Richard. 1985. War, nuclear war, and nuclear deterrence: Some conceptual and moral issues. *Ethics* 95:424–44.

Wendt, Alexander, and Raymond Duvall. 1989. Institutions and international order. In *Global changes and theoretical challenges: Approaches to world politics for the 1990s*, ed. Ernst-Otto Czempiel and James N. Rosenau, 51–73. Lexington, Mass.: Lexington Books.

Werner, Richard. 1987. The immorality of nuclear deterrence. In *Political realism and international morality*, ed. Kenneth Kipnis and Diana Meyers, 158–78. Boulder, Colo.: Westview Press.

White, Allan. 1975. *Modal thinking.* Ithaca, N.Y.: Cornell University Press.

Wolf, Susan. 1986. Self-interest and interest in selves. *Ethics* 96:704–20.

Wolfers, Arnold. 1962. *Discord and collaboration.* Baltimore: Johns Hopkins University Press.

Index

About the Author

Felix E. Oppenheim, professor emeritus of political science at the University of Massachusetts at Amherst, is the author of *Dimensions of Freedom* (1961), *Moral Principles in Political Philosophy* (1968), and *Political Concepts: A Reconstruction* (1981). He has contributed to the *International Encyclopedia of the Social Sciences,* the *Handbook of Political Science, Nomos,* and has published articles in various political science and philosophy journals. He has been the recipient of Guggenheim, Rockefeller, and Fulbright fellowships, and has lectured at various American, British, and Italian universities.